A Bite-Sized B...

Sex and
Critic.., Global
Perspectives

Edited by
Sue Joseph and Richard Lance Keeble

Published by Bite-Sized Books Ltd 2019

Bite-Sized Books Ltd Cleeve Croft, Cleeve Road, Goring RG8 9BJ UK
information@bite-sizedbooks.com
Registered in the UK. Company Registration No: 9395379

Bite-Sized Books Ltd Cleeve Croft, Cleeve Road, Goring RG8 9BJ UK
information@bite-sizedbooks.com
Registered in the UK. Company Registration No: 9395379
ISBN: 9781695107212

The editors

A journalist for more than forty years, working in Australia and the UK, Sue Joseph (PhD) began working as an academic, teaching print journalism at the University of Technology Sydney in 1997. As a Senior Lecturer, she now teaches in creative writing, particularly creative nonfiction writing, in both undergraduate and postgraduate programmes. Her research interests are around sexuality, secrets and confession, framed by the media, ethics and trauma narrative, memoir, reflective professional practice, ethical HDR supervision; nonfiction poetry and Australian creative nonfiction. Her fourth book, *Behind the Text: Candid Conversations with Australian Creative Nonfiction Writers*, was released in 2016. She is currently Joint Editor of *Ethical Space: The International Journal of Communication Ethics*.

Richard Lance Keeble is Professor of Journalism at the University of Lincoln and Honorary Professor at Liverpool Hope University. He has written and edited 40 books on a wide range of media-related subjects. The chair of the Orwell Society, he is the joint editor of *Ethical Space: The International Journal of Communication Ethics* and *George Orwell Studies*. In 2011, he gained a National Teaching Fellowship, the highest award for teachers in Higher Education in the UK, and in 2014 he was given a Lifetime Achievement Award by the Association for Journalism Education. In 2020, Routledge are to publish a collection of his essays under the title, *Journalism Beyond Orwell*.

Contents

Introduction

Breaking the Silence on Sexuality

Sue Joseph and Richard Lance Keeble

Is it not extraordinary that while sex features so prominently in the media the academy has given it so little attention? As far as we can establish, this is the first book of its kind devoted entirely to examining journalists' representation of sex. The coverage of 'negative' manifestations of sexuality – such as rape and sex trafficking – has been the focus of some considerable analysis, particularly by feminists such as Lisa M. Cuklanz (2000), Weidlein-Crist (2009), Nickie D. Phillips (2017) and Mendes, Ringrose and Keller (2019). And these important topics are not ignored in this volume. Sex scandals are also the focus of study – for instance, in Wilkes (2002) and Kinservik (2007). But look for texts on journalism's representation of love-making (in all its many manifestations) and you will find very little.

Perhaps it's all the result of the essential puritanism (and the frowning by conventional religions on bodily joy) that still pervades our cultures. So, significantly, the internationally focused *Ethical Reporting of Sensitive Issues*, edited by Anne Luce (2019), has a chapter on covering child sexual abuse but nothing on love-making (which is clearly far too sensitive). *The Sexuality of Men*, edited by Andy Metcalf and Martin Humphries (1985) has a chapter titled, invitingly, 'Male sexuality in the media', by Richard Dyer (ibid: 28-43). But it focuses on the symbolism of male sexuality being overwhelmingly centred on the genitals, particularly the penis, and the ambivalences surrounding male sexuality as represented in comedies such as the *Carry On* films and Benny Hill shows (now no longer shown in the UK).

There are significant exceptions, of course. In *Voices of Revolution: The Dissident Press in America*, Rodger Streitmatter (2001) devotes a chapter to exploring the (largely forgotten) history and content of progressive, free love journals in late 19th century America. These included the *Woodhull & Claflin's Weekly*, Moses Harman's *Lucifer, the Light-Bearer* and Ezra and Angela Heywood's *The Word*. Streitmatter concludes, arguing that 'these defiant women and men paid an exorbitant price for their dissidence. They dared Victorian society to rethink its view on sexual behavior despite censure, repression, denunciation, and the dark shadow of public disgrace' (ibid: 78). Gauntlett (2008: 164-222) traces the influences of magazines on the formation of modern masculinities and female identities; Fisher, Hill, Grube and Gruber (2007) look at the gay, lesbian and bisexual content on television; while more recently the representation of sexuality on the internet has become the focus for some important research as, for instance, in van Doorn, Wyatt and van Zoonen (2012).

Critical Overviews: Setting the Scene

One of the many problems linked to the reporting of sexuality across the globe is that there is no media speciality (or 'beat') linked prominently to the field – unlike, say, defence, health, politics, sports, religion, environment. Nor is there any clear definition of 'sex journalism'. But this does not mean that the term 'sex journalist' is completely unknown. In the UK, for instance, Alix Fox defines herself as one (see Kale 2018). In Australia, too, there are a number of sex journalists. In our opening chapter, Belinda Middleweek notes that sex, significantly, is not mentioned in Galtung and Ruge's foundational, 1965 study of news values. She comments: 'The varying and disputed status of sex in news value taxonomies is one explanation for the few definitions of sex journalism that exist and, more broadly, the lack of debate about sex journalism as a distinct news genre.'

In order to establish what sex journalism is, Middleweek goes on to interview 10 freelances specialising in the field to find out their views. The responses, as one can imagine, are varied and often eye-opening. Some, for instance, were 'warned by mentors such as journalism academics and news industry professionals to avoid sex journalism because of its perceived low news status'. The fact that it's women who tend to be drawn to sex journalism largely accounts for this low status. Middleweek concludes: 'In her call for sex journalism to be taken seriously, one interviewee asks: "When does the first sex journalist win a Pulitzer?" My answer? Never in this pink ghetto.'

Also taking a critical overview of the field, Matthew Ricketson surveys the foundational texts of literary journalism and wonders why love-making features so rarely in them: 'Sex is certainly included in works of literary journalism but rarely as a simple act of pleasure or procreation and much more often in its aberrant or abhorrent forms.' The difficulty of sourcing the material maybe behind this silence, he ponders: 'First-hand observation of events is a staple of literary

4

journalism; being a fly-on-the-wall is commonly invoked as a term of praise. But a fly-on-the-bedsheets? That sounds ludicrous.'

Descriptions of love-making sometimes appear in memoirs. But Ricketson is particularly impressed by a piece of reportage beyond the boundaries of literary journalism: namely *Bonk: The Curious Coupling of Science and Sex* by science journalist Mary Roach who 'seems intent on filling any gaps left after Woody Allen's 1972 film *Everything You Wanted to Know About Sex But were Afraid to Ask*'. And a joint biography of the sex researchers, William Masters and Virginia Johnson by Thomas Maier (2009) 'offers at least a pathway for literary journalists to write about sex and love-making'.

Global, Critical Perspectives

As a survivor of sexual assault, Saxon Mullins's right to anonymity is, by Australian law, set in stone. But, on 6 May 2018, she decided to go public. In the first of our case studies, Sue Joseph analyses in depth the *Four Corners* broadcast which led to the New South Wales Attorney General referring the state's consent laws to the NSW Law Reform Commission. Joseph stresses: 'The effectiveness of the *Four Corners* format is that the audience is given access, albeit guided by the reporter, to the people involved. We watch Saxon Mullins discuss her experience. We see her attempt to control her emotions; we see true consequences of trauma on her face and in the way she holds her body. We even get to hear her empathic response to sending another young person to jail.'

Karley Sciortino and Jessica Valenti are journalists who dare to appropriate normally pejorative terms such as 'slut' and 'sex object' to promote progressive notions about gender and sexuality. Here, Kylie Cardell and Emma Maguire examine their writings but do not evade the complexities, arguing: 'In effect, Valenti and Sciortino demand to have it both ways – to sell themselves as sex objects and use this marketability professionally to critique dominant power structures. This tension begs us to ask whether, ultimately, trading on these labels is buying into a cultural agreement about the oppression at the root of this language. Maybe it is, but it is also why we must listen to these writers who are challenging so bravely the public discourses that oppress and shame feminine sexuality.'

The spotlight shifts to Lydia Cacho who has spent her entire career investigating the ways social, political and economic systems create, perpetuate and benefit from the international sex market – and she has

5

done so at great personal cost. Todd Schack outlines her unique reporting style. This, he argues, blends first-person narratives with investigative journalism techniques and, avoiding moral condemnation, presents a political-economy analysis, highlighting the consequences of neoliberalism and the economic factors driving international market of sex slavery. Moreover, Cacho studiously allows the exploited women and girls space to speak for themselves. For Schack, 'Lydia Cacho is, indeed, a model for anyone who wishes to become a journalist: she is a warrior for the cause and she will not be silenced'.

Child sexual abuse is now relatively common in the news. But, as Claire Konkes argues in her chapter on sex crimes and cover-ups, journalists must grapple with the complexity and ambiguity in these stories to avoid sensationalist coverage. Konkes also considers the controversial subject of 'conspiracy theories' which often accompany sex crimes and suggests they 'can be locations for investigating how effectively the powerful attempt to influence public debate and, in turn, how effectively news media represent or challenge the communication strategies of the powerful'.

Ethical issues are also in the forefront of Julie Wheelwright's chapter which follows. In 2016, Gay Talese, the eminent American literary journalist, published *The Voyeur's Motel* based on the journals of a self-confessed voyeur – involving copulation, drug dealing, incest and even murder. Not surprisingly, a massive controversy erupted. Wheelwright, in examining the issues, criticises Talese's self-reflective mode in the book for failing to address fully concerns about consent and transparency. And Wheelwright ends with this useful piece of advice: 'Perhaps the most vital message in this exploration into reporting on the fraught territory of sexual intimacy is the need for psychological insight and an ability to face up to the raw honesty of our motivating psyches.'

The spotlight shifts to Mexico where a collective of sex workers, infuriated by the social and media stigmatisation, have turned to journalism to tell their own stories. After seven years of dedicated training, their book, *Whores, Journalist and Activists*, has been published. According to Antonio Castillo, the book has 'deeply empowered' the sex workers. 'They see themselves as historical subjects able to reclaim the word "whore" as a fighting banner in the struggle for their human rights. And they have been also able to recognise the agency that journalism and activism together have in demanding respect, acceptance and recognition.'

Next, Manuel Coutinho examines the role journalism played in confronting the taboos surrounding homosexuality in Portugal during the 1980s when the conservative mores of the Salazar dictatorship (1932-1968) were persisting. In particular, he considers the brave reporting of Guilherme de Melo in the short-lived journal *Cadernos de Reportagem*.

In his chapter on literary journalism in the opening section, Matthew Ricketson highlights the rather gross depiction of rape as told by 'Charlie' at the start of George Orwell's first book, the part memoir/part fictional *Down and Out in Paris and London* (1933). Indeed, while Orwell is generally associated with the dystopian gloom and doom of *Nineteen Eighty-Four* (1949), there was a life-affirmative side to both his character and writings – and sexuality was very much part of that, as Richard Lance Keeble argues. Thus, the role of sex in works as diverse as *Homage to Catalonia* (1938), his account of fighting alongside Republican militiamen in the Spanish civil war, the part memoir/part fictional 'Such, Such were the Joys' (1952) and his *Horizon*, celebratory essay on the sexy seaside postcards of Donald McGill (1941) is considered.

Finally in this section, Anna Hoyles explores the ways in which sexuality and its consequences become a metaphor for the class struggle in the journalism of the Swedish working class writer, Moa Martinson (1890-1964). In particular, she looks closely at two examples of Martinson's work: one a sober look at the consequences of a lack of contraception and education, and the other a light-hearted satire on the sexual mores of the middle and upper classes.

Hoyles concludes: 'Despite the very different tone of the two types of writing discussed, they share similar ideas. For Martinson, the injustice of the class system and of gender imbalance, and the need for solidarity and new ways of thinking are perennial themes.'

In the brief Conclusion, the editors argue that sex is one the 'few final societal taboos that journalists and academics need to make more commonplace to report on, discuss and evaluate'.

References

Cucklanz, Lisa M. (2000) *Rape on Prime Time: Television, Masculinity and Sexual Violence*, Philadelphia: University of Pennsylvania Press

Fisher, Deborah A., Hill, Douglas, L., Grube, Joel, W. and Gruber, Enid L. (2007) Gay, lesbian and bisexual content on television, *Journal of Homosexuality*, Vol. 52, Nos 3 and 4 pp 167-188

Gauntlett, David (2008) *Media, Gender and Identity: An Introduction*, Abingdon, Oxon: Routledge

Kale, Sirin (2018) Working as a sex journalist taught me when to say no, Alex Fox interviewed, *Vice*, 13 September. Available online at https://www.vice.com/en_us/article/mbwjzn/working-as-sex-journalist-alix-fox, accessed on 30 July 2019

Kinservik, Matthew (2007) *Sex, Scandal and Celebrity in Late Eighteen-Century England*, Basingstoke, Palgrave MacMillan

Mendes, Kaitlynn, Ringrose, Jessica and Keller, Jessalynn (2019) *Digital Feminist Activism: Girls and Women Fight Back Against Rape Culture*, Oxford: Oxford University Press

Phillips, Nickie D. (2017) *Rape Culture in Popular Media*, Lanham, Maryland: Rowman and Littlefield

Streitmatter, Rodger (2001) *Voices of Revolution: The Dissident Press in America*, New York: Columbia University Press

Van Dorn, Niels, Wyatt, Sally and van Zoonen, Liesbet (2012) A body of the text: Revisiting textual performances of gender and sexuality on the internet, Kearney, Mary Celeste (ed.) *The Gender and Media Reader*, New York, Abingdon, Oxon: Routledge

Weidlein-Crist, Philisa J. (2009) *The Media's Treatment of Sexual Assault by Athletes in a Post-Rape Reform Era*, Delaware, University of Delaware Press

Wilkes, Roger (2002) *Scandal: A Scurrilous History of Gossip*, London: Atlantic Books

Chapter 1

'In a pink ghetto': How Female News Workers Define Sex Journalism

What precisely is sex journalism? Belinda Middleweek interviews 10 freelances specialising in the field to find out. And she concludes that if, as researchers agree, the accurate coverage of sex could well improve people's sexual health, a greater understanding of the professional identities of sex journalists will go some way towards that goal.

The #MeToo movement has prompted broader public discussion about the construction of sexual identities and practices in media (Gill and Orgad 2018: 1314). Despite greater prominence and the personal, public and political relevance of the study of human sexuality (McBride et al. 2007), little research exists on the journalists whose specialty is to report on sexual matters. In the research that does exist, the motivations of news workers are considered questionable since journalists 'generally do not value sex as a topic', they receive 'scarce formal training' and their reporting evidences 'a lack of evidence-based content and critical questioning' (Boynton and Callaghan 2006: 334; see also McBride et.al. 2007).

These views are also commonplace among 'sexperts' such as sex educators, sexual health clinicians and therapists with whom sex journalists may share aspects of their work practices. In one of the few studies of the source-journalist relationship on this topic, sexperts believed media coverage of sex was intended to 'sensationalize, titillate, or create controversy' (McBride et.al. 2007: 351). In another, sexperts were described as being frustrated by the limited range of sex news coverage and the difficulty they had persuading journalists of alternate viewpoints (Boynton and Callaghan 2006: 336).

Yet there is an increasing number of news workers self-identifying as 'sex journalists' and 'sex writers' in their news articles and blog posts. The nomenclature suggests theirs is a special 'beat' of journalism, much like court reporters whose niche is crime and policing, or sports journalists with cultivated expertise in matters both on and off the field. To explore this trend further and address the lack of research on practitioner perspectives of sex news, I conducted in-depth interviews with 10 sex journalists from the US (6), Canada (1), Germany (1) and Australia (2) – all of them female freelances writing for mainstream news media, digital-only publications and on their own blog sites.

Initially, recruitment involved an online Google news search of 'sex and journalism' to compile a list of prominent journalists writing about sex, but the majority were interviewed based on the recommendations of existing study participants in a form of snowball sampling. Though only modest in size and not a representative sample of all sex journalists, the news worker insights gathered here offer a compelling picture of sex journalism and the views and perceptions of news workers whose number is in line with other academic studies of practitioner perspectives (see Deuze 2005) and described as 'a small but strategically important group' (Kunelius and Ruusunoksa 2008).

The broad aim of this chapter is to trace the origins of sex news, define and situate sex journalism in a gendered news niche and, through participant responses, consider the professional identities of sex journalists. The following research questions will be investigated in this chapter: what is sex journalism and is gender a factor in the construction of sex journalists' professional identities? Situating the present study of sex journalists in the socio-cultural context of #MeToo activism and amid calls for the reframing of sex discourse by media and sexuality scholars (Hatley Major and Walker 2010), opens up important dialogue about sex and points to the role of media in disseminating sex information, education and advice. But firstly, what is sex journalism – and is sex news?

What is Sex Journalism?

The prominence of sex in mass market publications such as Britain's *Daily Mirror* and its rival the *Sun* would indicate sex is newsworthy, the latter earning its owner Rupert Murdoch the dubious title of purveyor of 'bonk journalism' (McNair 1994: 145-146). Indeed, the question of sex – as a news value at least – has aroused debate since the 1930s when Curtis MacDougall published his nine-volume textbook *Interpretive Reporting* (1938) that set the tone and shaped debate about journalism education for half a century (Stovall 1990: 28). MacDougall includes sex in his taxonomy of news values which accords some status to the term, though he links sex to the news factor of 'age' in at least three of those nine volumes (MacDougall in Parks 2018: 15). MacDougall's work is among 75 journalism textbooks by 50 first authors whom Perry Parks analyses in his impressive, longitudinal study of journalists' conceptions of news and news value development throughout more than a century of practice. Sex appears variably in the journalism textbooks sampled as both an independent news value and a sub-category of human interest (ibid). Though not among the seven core news values identified in the study – namely timeliness, proximity, prominence, unusualness, impact, human interest and conflict – sex appears frequently in Parks's historical sample and that, he says, is a more valuable indicator of significance than the discreteness of any one term (ibid: 19, 14). As a news value, sex is also recognised by former *Guardian* editor Alastair Hetherington who includes the term in his news values criteria arising from a study of UK newspapers in the 1980s (Hetherington 1985: 8-9), as does Herbert twenty years later in his eight-point list of elements guiding the news selection process (Herbert 2000: 318).

Somewhat surprisingly, given the longstanding issue, sex is absent from Galtung and Ruge's (1965) list of 12 news values in a study that has been the mainstay of journalism research for more than 50 years, republished in edited collections by Tunstall (1970), Cohen and Young (1973) and Tumber (1999) and validated by others as the foundational study of news values (Bell 1991; Palmer 1998 cited in Harcup and O'Neill 2001: 4). In their review of Galtung and Ruge's work, Harcup and O'Neill argue the absence of sex is a limitation of the study for the reason that sex is 'an important factor in contemporary news values' and should be added to existing classifications (ibid: 14).

The varying and disputed status of sex in news value taxonomies is one explanation for the few definitions of sex journalism that exist and, more broadly, the lack of debate about sex journalism as a distinct news genre. Among those few studies that do exist, sex journalism is defined according to different parameters. McBride et al. define what they call 'sex news' by topic coverage, framed as research about sexuality, sexual behaviour and sexual health. By contrast, Mark McLelland locates sex journalism (or *sei jānarizumu*) historically in the 'upsurge in sexual discourse' in the Japanese *kasutori* (the 'dregs') or 'sex press' of the 1940s and 50s (2012: 6) that is evident in the increased discussion of sex and erotic material in popular newspapers,

11

magazines and even journals targeting a middle-brow readership (ibid: 61, 78).

Varying definitions of sex journalism also characterise the interviews conducted for this study. As with McBride et al., some provide a list of topics to define sex journalism as 'sex, health, dating, business trends' (Interviewee 4) and 'sex, relationships, psychology, fashion, beauty, sexual orientation, mental health and improvement' (Interviewee 3), while others confidently narrow the domain to a 'collective interest in the topic of sexuality' (Interviewee 1) or 'It's about health and relationships' (Interviewee 8). Some define sex journalism using 'quality' indicators that are described as either 'science work' or the more tabloid '*Cosmo* fluff' (in reference to the popular women's glossy magazine *Cosmopolitan*) as typified in the advice stories '10 ways to make him harder' or '[How] to be a temptress in bed' (Interviewee 2). That view is echoed in another interviewee's remarks about the limited publication alternatives for sex journalists who could either 'sell shit to *Cosmo* or serious to *Slate*' (Interviewee 4). The desire for and aspiration to quality sex journalism – or at least to be taken seriously as journalists who write about sex – is expressed by all those interviewed for this study.

Occupational Ideology of Sex Journalists

Some attribute 'quality' in sex journalism to a 'journalistic perspective' (Interviewee 5) while their ideal-typical values are consistent with research on journalism's shared occupational ideology of public service, objectivity, independence, immediacy and ethics (Deuze 2005a). Others argue sex journalism is informed by literary movements of the 1960s such as 'new journalism' as well as 'creative nonfiction' (Interviewees 1 and 3) and 'narrative nonfiction journalism' (Interviewee 4) that provide 'input' and writing inspiration. For the interviewees concerned, those literary genres had in common with sex journalism the frequent use of first-person point-of-view 'where the writer involves themselves in some way' in the story (Interviewee 3) by acting as the 'journalist emissary into another world' (Interviewee 6). Since readers 'have a lot of curiosity about worlds unfamiliar to them', they believe sex journalists provide an experiential and what is often an 'experimental' perspective in their reporting: whether that is 'trying out a crazy new sex toy' or 'going to an erotic dinner party' (Interviewee 6).

One interviewee shares an eagerness to leave her legacy as 'The Hunter S. Thompson of sex writing', envisioning her role as 'Virgil to the readers' Dante' (Interviewee 4). Not all agree that subjectivity or the use of a 'personal bent' (Interviewee 5) in journalism is a requirement or even desirable for the reason that 'anecdata' and 'first person accounts won't effect change' (Interviewee 8). Those who agree with the use of first-person accounts in sex journalism also describe being called to the profession ('driven into this work because of personal questions I wanted answered' or 'it chose me' – Interviewees 3 and 6) and were 'warned' by mentors such as journalism academics and news industry professionals to avoid sex journalism because of its perceived low news status (Interviewees 3 and 6).

Given the varying opinion among interviewees about both the breadth of topics constituting sex journalism and its journalistic style, a more useful definition of sex journalism is founded on an agreed occupational ideology that does not always involve the exercise of journalistic objectivity (Deuze 2005a) but does entail an empathetic skill set. The majority of interviewees agree that sex journalists require a 'sense of empathy' (Interviewees 5 and 1) because 'there's still a lot of shame around sex' (Interviewee 5) and 'you have to feel less shame' (Interviewee 10), sources are 'vulnerable' (Interviewee 1), 'you encounter things that are gross and weird or upsetting' (Interviewee 3) and 'people are going to tell you the craziest things' (Interviewee 4). For others, this same quality is expressed as a 'bodies and relationships skill set' (Interviewee 9) that is sensitive not only to the sexual orientations of sources and the use of correct gender pronouns and binaries in reportage but also the journalist's own position of privilege as storyteller (Interviewees 1 and 4).

Boundary work is also an ideal-typical value shared by the sex journalists interviewed. This finding is consistent with research on the professional norms and values of journalists of all stripes among whom the use of 'boundary markers' provides distinction between journalists and non-journalists in online environments (Singer in Carlson and Lewis 2015). For the interviewees in this study, however, boundary work is an exercise in personal and professional safety. One interviewee explains: 'You have to constantly make your own boundaries known' (Interviewee 5) and often that occurs on the job. Others describe the 'war correspondent mentality' (Interviewees 1 and 4) that comes with this form of news work in which 'your mental state and your body [are] on the line in the pursuit of a story' (Interviewee

4), while another describes the 'extreme risks' that arise from the fact that 'people hate women' and men tend to ask: 'Are you that slut who wrote about ... whatever' (Interviewee 10). Another interprets boundary work as an exercise in self-restraint: 'If [the topic] is something that turns you on then you need to take a step back' (Interviewee 2), and there is overwhelming agreement that writing about sex often leads audiences to assume the sexual promiscuity of the reporter. Though beyond the scope of the present study, the precarity and risk typifying the practice of sex journalism is worthy of further consideration.

Based on these interviewee reflections, sex journalism is defined as a collective interest in the topic of sexuality that is reported in a factual and timely manner with regard for the social and ethical considerations of journalism practice and the values of open-mindedness, empathy and boundary-setting. Rather than defined by subject matter or journalistic style, this more expansive definition follows in the tradition of defining journalism according to news values and professional standards of newsmaking (see Deuze 2005a; Deuze and Witschge 2018) that are cultivated by journalists who write about sex.

A Pink Ghetto

Among all study participants, sex journalism is regarded as a female news niche or 'pink ghetto' (Interviewee 1), summarised in one interviewee's reflection: 'When I think about sex journalism, I don't think of any men' (Interviewee 6). Though one suggests sex journalism be democratised since 'there should be a collective understanding of how to orgasm', that interviewee also adds the caveat: 'There are some things you have to have the equipment to understand' (Interviewee 8). Two interviewees took umbrage at the very thought of male sex journalists, describing them as a 'pet peeve' because their writing is usually 'masturbatory or leering' (Interviewee 7) or because of scepticism about their motivations and the personal 'safety' concerns (read: distrust) of 'sex writing from dudes' (Interviewee 10). As such, sex journalism constitutes for the study participants a discourse of exceptionalism for women that is consistent with research that finds 'sex coverage is gendered' and often reported by female freelances (Boynton and Callaghan 2006: 341).

However, the knitting of women and sex journalism carries certain historical and gendered assumptions about declining news quality, professional values and journalistic standards. For Karen Ross and

Cynthia Carter in their compelling research for the Global Media Monitoring project, issues and topics relevant to women are relegated to the margins of news because of 'male-defined news selection criteria' suggesting 'what is of interest to women is less important than that which interests men...' (Ross and Carter 2011: 1109). Those topics are elsewhere defined as '... women's health, family and childcare, sexual harassment and discrimination, rape and battering, homeless mothers, quality of life and other social issues' (Marzolf 1993 in Chambers et al. 91).

The prestige accorded to hard news compared with its 'lighter' or 'soft' counterpart is, the research tells us, a result of men's monopolised reporting of public affairs, politics and war (Steiner in Allan 2005: 42) and carries the assumption that women's everyday lives were 'intrinsically less "newsworthy" as a result' (Allan 1998: 133 cited in Ross and Carter 2011: 1149). Laments about declining standards of hard news (or 'quality journalism') are challenged by a number of media scholars who argue that soft news and its attendant 'tabloid practices' (e.g. the personalisation of news) achieves an 'opening up of public discourse' allowing a multitude of voices to be heard (Bird 2000: 219; see also Lumby 1999; Turner 2004; Middleweek 2007), as well as making accessible to a news reading public, more abstract or complex issues (Bird 2000; MacDonald 1998).

Understanding the symbolic association of women with so-called soft news topics that are routinely reported by sex journalists and considered 'lightweight' and 'the least important feature' (Boynton and Callaghan 2006: 341) not only locates this type of news work in gendered discourses but also points to the value system informing the professional identities of practitioners. That value system certainly informs the experiences of sex journalists in this study who describe the 'stigma and shame' of reporting sex (Interviewees 9 and 10), 'not [being] taken as seriously' in their profession (Interviewees 1, 6 and 10), amid the prevailing assumption that sex journalism is 'the lowest hanging fruit ... and devalued as a result' (Interviewee 6). Nearly all use variations of the terms 'pigeonhole' and 'pink ghetto' to describe the professional limitations of specialising in sex reportage.

Conclusion
The mainstream media's reporting of #MeToo suggests journalism about sexual practices and behaviour is no longer confined to fringe publications, so-called 'smutty' news providers or tabloids. As

interviewees describe, '#Metoo raises a lot of questions about the nuances of sexual interaction to a degree we haven't seen before' (Interviewee 6), occasioned the 'wholesale redefining of gender, desire, sexual orientation and behaviours' (Interviewee 4) and 'opened up a conversation and awareness about sex' (Interviewee 9). That increased awareness and attention to sexual matters, combined with a number of journalists specialising in news writing about sex, necessitates a definition of sex journalism that recognises both its domain specialty and the ideal-typical values held by practitioners.

While based on a small sample of practitioner interviews, the definition offered here is an attempt to chart that territory. Even though there is little consensus on the topics covered by sex journalists or its distinctive style, in highlighting the specialist skill set of journalists who write about sex, the majority of interviewees identify sex journalism as a discernible news niche. That 'active construction of distinction' (Deuze 2005b: 879) coincides with findings of a study of Dutch tabloid journalists whose professional identities pivot on the distinguishing of their news work in an increasingly hybridised news environment.

Interviewees also point to gender as a key factor in the comparatively low status of sex journalism and the greater risks involved in its practice. As one exclaims: 'Women end up exploring these issues more because so often the people impacted are women ... and it's the women who are exploited' (Interviewee 2). If, as researchers agree, the 'accurate and well-articulated' coverage of sex could 'improve sexual health and enhance individual lives' (McBride et al. 2007: 348), a greater understanding of the professional identities of sex journalists will go some way towards that goal. But more positive sexual health outcomes do not guarantee wider acceptance of those who report sex. In her call for sex journalism to be taken seriously, one interviewee asks: 'When does the first sex journalist win a Pulitzer?' (Interviewee 4). My answer? Never in this pink ghetto.

References

Bell, Allan (1991) *The Language of News Media*, Oxford: Blackwell

Bird, S. Elizabeth (2000) Audience demands in a murderous market: Tabloidization in US television news, Sparks, Colin and Tulloch, John (eds) *Tabloid Tales: Global Debates Over Media Standards*, Oxford: Roman & Littlefield Publishers pp 213-228

Boynton, Petra M. and Callaghan, Will (2006) Understanding media coverage of sex: A practical discussion paper for sexologists and journalists, *Sexual and Relationship Therapy*, Vol. 21, No.3 pp 333-346

Chambers, Deborah, Steiner, Linda and Fleming, Carole (2004) *Women and Journalism*, London, New York: Routledge

Cohen, Stanley and Young, Jock (1973) *The Manufacture of News: A Reader*, London: Sage Publications

Deuze, Mark (2005a) What is journalism? Professional identity and ideology of journalists reconsidered. *Journalism*, Vol 6, No. 4 pp 443–465

Deuze, Mark (2005b) Popular journalism and professional ideology: Tabloid reporters and editors speak out, *Media, Culture and Society*, Vol. 27, No. 6 pp 861-882

Deuze, Mark and Witschge, Tamara (2018) Beyond journalism: Theorizing the transformation of journalism, *Journalism*. Vol. 19 No. 2 pp 165-181

Galtung, Johan and Ruge, Mari (1965) The structure of foreign news: The presentation of the Congo, Cuba and Cyprus Crises in four Norwegian newspapers, *Journal of International Peace Research*, Vol. 2 pp 64-90

Gill, Rosalind and Orgad, Shani (2018) The shifting terrain of sex and power: From the 'sexualization of culture' to #MeToo, *Sexualities*, Vol. 21, No. 8 pp 1313-1324

Harcup, Tony and O'Neill, Deirdre (2001) What Is news? Galtung and Ruge revisited, *Journalism Studies*, Vol.2, No.2 pp 261-280

Hatley Major, Lesa and Walker, Kimberly K. (2010) Newspapers lack substantive reporting on sexual issues, *Newspaper Research Journal*, Vol. 31, No. 4 (Fall) pp 62-76

Herbert, John (2000) *Journalism in the Digital Age*, Oxford: Focal Press

Hetherington, Alastair (1985) *News, Newspapers and Television*, London: Macmillan

Kunelius, Risto and Ruusunoksa, Laura (2008) Mapping professional imagination, *Journalism Studies*, Vol.9, No.5 pp 662-678

Lumby, Catharine (1999) *Gotcha: Life in a Tabloid World*, Sydney: Allen & Unwin

MacDonald, Myra (1998) Politicizing the personal: Women's voices in British television documentary, Carter, Cynthia, Branston, Gillian and Allan, Stuart (eds) *News, Gender and Power*, London: Routledge pp 105-120

McBride, Kimberly R., Sanders, Stephanie A., Janssen, Erick, Grabe, Maria Elizabeth, Bass, Jennifer, Sparks, Johnny V., Brown, Trevor R. and Heiman, Julia R. (2007) Turning sexual science into news: Sex research and the media, *Journal of Sex Research*, Vol. 44, No.4 pp 347-358

McNair, Brian (1994) *News and Journalism in the UK: A Textbook*, London: Routledge

McLelland, Mark (2012) *Love, Sex and Democracy in Japan during the American Occupation*, New York: Palgrave MacMillan

Middleweek, Belinda (2007) *Dingo Media? R v Chamberlain as Model for an Australian Media Event*. PhD thesis, University of Sydney

Parks, Perry (2018) Textbook news values: Stable concepts, changing choices, *Journalism & Mass Communication Quarterly*. Available online at https://doi.org/10.1177/1077699018805212

Ross, Karen and Carter, Cynthia (2011) Women and news: A long and winding road, *Media, Culture & Society*, Vol. 33, No.8 pp 1148–1165

Singer, Jane B. (2015) Out of bounds: Professional norms as boundary markers, Carlson, Matt and Lewis, Seth C. (eds) *Boundaries of Journalism: Professionalism, Practices and Participation*, London, New York: Routledge pp 21-36

Steiner, Linda (2005) The 'gender matters' debate in journalism: Lessons from the front, Allan, Stuart (ed.) *Journalism: Critical Issues*, Berkshire, England, Open University Press pp 42-53

Stovall, James Glen (1990) The practitioners, Sloan, W. David (ed.) *Makers of the Media Mind: Journalism Educators and their Ideas*, New York, London: Routledge pp 23-58

Tumber, Howard (ed.) (1999) *Journalism: Critical Concepts in Media and Cultural Studies*, London: Routledge

Tunstall, Jeremy (ed.) (1970) *Media Sociology: A Reader*, London: Constable

Turner, Graeme (2004) *Understanding Celebrity*, London: Sage Publications

Note on the Author

Belinda Middleweek is a Senior Lecturer at the University of Technology Sydney, Australia. Her research focuses on news media constructions of gender as well as mediations and technologies of intimacy. She is the author of *Real Sex Films: The New Intimacy and Risk in Cinema* (2017 OUP, with John Tulloch).

Chapter 2

The Fly-on-the-Bedsheets: Literary Journalism and the Portrayal of Love-Making

Matthew Ricketson wonders why sex features so rarely in most of the leading texts of literary journalism – but he discovers a few notable exceptions including one titled *Bonk*.

One of the great promises – and appeals – of literary journalism is that it tells true stories about events and issues in their complexity and people in their full humanity. Literary journalists take readers to all parts of the globe, from high society life in one of the world's great cities (the Bernsteins' fund-raising party for the Black Panthers in Tom Wolfe's *Radical Chic*, of 1970) to the discovery of terrifying viruses in the remotest parts of Africa (Richard Preston's *The Hot Zone*, of 1994). They peel away the intricacies of the everyday (John McPhee's *Oranges*, 1967) and reveal what those in power have fought hard to hide (Louise Milligan's *Cardinal: The Rise and Fall of George Pell*, 2017). They help us see the human faces buried in historic events (Martha Gellhorn's *The View from the Ground*, 1988) and remind us of the extraordinary in ordinary people's lives (Tracy Kidder's *Among Schoolchildren*, 1989). There are signature works of literary journalism about almost every area of life: war (John Hersey's *Hiroshima*, 1946); politics (Hunter S. Thompson's *Fear and Loathing on the Campaign Trail '72*, 1973); sport (Madeleine Blais's *In These Girls, Hope is a Muscle*, 1995); crime (Truman Capote's *In Cold Blood*, 1965); business (Jane Mayer's *Dark Money*, 2016); the environment (Rachel Carson's *Silent Spring*, 1962); the law (Ted Conover's *Newjack*, 2000); the media (Janet Malcolm's *The Journalist and the Murderer*, 1989); religion (Lawrence Wright's *Going Clear*, 2013), and work (Barbara Ehrenreich's *Nickel and Dimed*, 2001).

In the introduction to *Literary Journalism*, Norman Sims writes: 'At a time when journalism seems crowded with celebrities, literary journalism pays respect to ordinary lives. Literary journalists write narratives focused on everyday events that bring out the hidden patterns of community life as tellingly as the spectacular stories that make newspaper headlines' (1995: 3).

Why, then, are there so few accounts in literary journalism of ordinary people's love lives? Why, especially, when making love is one of the most joyous and powerful experiences a person can have, and literary journalism as a genre, unlike straight news, brims over with vivid portrayals of powerful and joyous experiences? These questions prompted the writing of this chapter. Just consider the works listed above: how many contain portraits, or even descriptions, of people's love lives? The married life – but not the love life – of Lieutenant Colonel Nancy Jaax and Colonel Jerry Jaax is portrayed in *The Hot Zone* as it comes under pressure during the Reston biohazard operation that is central to Preston's 1994 book about the Ebola virus. Sex, or more to the point, sexual crimes, play a role in some of the works listed above: they are central to Milligan's investigative biography of Cardinal George Pell, recounting allegations of child sexual abuse for which Pell was later charged and convicted, in 2018 (and against which he is appealing). In *Newjack* and *In Cold Blood*, they are peripheral: in the former, Conover discusses sex and rape in prison briefly (2000: 261-265); and in the latter, Capote writes that Dick Hickock intended raping Nancy Clutter before killing her, though the rape allegation is contested (Ricketson 2014: 84-85).

Beyond the Sexual Crimes Syndrome

Sexual crimes, of course, are a common topic in true crime books, some of which, like Capote's path-finding 1965 text, *In Cold Blood*, have, or aspire to, literary merit, while others are sensationalist and pander to the voyeuristic impulse, as exemplified in Glyn Jones's *True Crime through History* (1989), an edited collection of excerpts from books about some truly horrific crimes that are gathered together in sections bearing titles like 'Classic crimes', 'The sick Sixties, and beyond' and 'Mass murderers, and more'. These titles are only one step short of the name given to the mock true crime television show featured in the 1993 film *Addams Family Values* – 'America's Most Disgusting Unsolved Crimes'.

Equally, if not more troubling, is literary journalism about sexual crimes, and sexuality, which is overtly voyeuristic. Gay Talese is an iconic figure in literary journalism circles but, as Julie Wheelwright demonstrates persuasively, the sexist assumptions and manipulative behaviour underlying *They Neighbor's Wife*, his 1980 book about sexual liberation, and more recently, his 2016 book, *The Voyeur's Motel*, mean Talese's reputation needs re-assessing (Wheelwright 2017, see also Chapter 7). In the latter book about a self-proclaimed voyeur who for many years spied on guests in the motel he runs with his wife in Denver, Colorado, Talese only half-heartedly questions the conduct of either Gerald Foos or himself. Instead, he makes the reader complicit in their joint voyeurism: 'I stretched my neck to the maximum in order to see as much as I could while peeking down through the vent (nearly butting heads with Foos as I did so) – and finally what I saw was....' (2016: 33). He goes on to provide detailed descriptions of people undressing, masturbating, and having sex; I'll spare you the details even if Talese doesn't. Most disturbingly, though, the book is written in a tone that wavers between dispassionate observation and sly erotica. It makes for uncomfortable reading, and not in a good way.

Love and love-making are core human experiences; the former features in many literary journalism texts, the latter in few. Similarly, sex is certainly included in works of literary journalism but rarely as a simple act of pleasure or procreation and much more often in its aberrant or abhorrent forms. What is this odd, rarely discussed element of literary journalism about? Is the predominance in literary journalism of sexual problems and crimes rather than simple sex or love-making a function of the maxim that conflict and drama drive stories? As Richard Holmes, respected biographer of numerous Romantic poets, asks: 'Where the mundane, in its richest sense, is central to a life – as in a happy marriage – it is often peculiarly impotent, both in its sources and in its narrative invention (how to describe twenty years of tender, ruminative breakfasts?)' (Holmes 1995: 19). Or, is the paucity of descriptions of love-making in literary journalism to do with the difficulty of sourcing the material? First-hand observation of events is a staple of literary journalism; being a fly-on-the-wall is commonly invoked as a term of praise. But a fly-on-the-bedsheets? It sounds ludicrous.

Perhaps both explanations are valid. The former – that it is a function of the maxim that conflict drives stories – is seen in two well-known historical examples of literary journalism: George Orwell's *Down and Out in Paris and London* and Gloria Steinem's 'I was a Playboy

Bunny'. The latter was feminist journalist Steinem's 1963 undercover participatory account of the sexism and oppressive working conditions experienced by women working in the Playboy clubs rather than the glamour and entrée to social success promised by the clubs' recruitment advertisements. Central to Steinem's long article, originally published in *Show* magazine, was not sex but the selling of women's sexual appeal. Published in 1933, *Down and Out in Paris and London* is Orwell's first book and is remembered best for his vivid account of working as a *plongeur* in Paris and surviving as a tramp in England. Less often commented on is his graphic account of sex in a brothel in Paris. 'Charlie', one of the rue de Coq d'Or's 'local curiosities', presents a tale of seduction after which Orwell comments only that Charlie was a 'curious specimen' (Orwell 1974 [1933] 12-14). What is actually described by Charlie, though, is what one of Orwell's biographers, Gordon Bowker (2003: 137), terms a 'sadistic rape' and another, D. J. Taylor, as a Parisian tall story that 'has clearly wandered in from some late-nineteenth century decadent's confessional' (Taylor 2003: 99).

Love-making and the Memoir

The latter explanation – that the paucity of scenes of love-making is to do with the difficulty of sourcing the material – demonstrates why we are more likely to read such accounts in autobiographical texts where it is the writer's decision to include – or not – accounts of love-making. Kate Holden made her reputation in Australia through a remarkable 2005 memoir, *In My Skin*, recounting in grittily intimate detail her time as a heroin addict and sex worker and then, in simply intimate detail, her love life, in a second volume of memoir, *The Romantic: Italian Nights and Days*, of 2010.

Of her sex work, she writes: 'I remember opening my heart to strange men and stroking their faces, smiling. I remember being pounded so hard my face was white with pain' (2005: 1). These sentences may not be easy to read – certainly Holden's father found them confronting, as she tells Sue Joseph in an interview (2016: 78-79), but that is a choice the writer made.

Going Too Far *In the Garden?*

Such considerations are evident in John Berendt's *Midnight in the Garden of Good and Evil* (1994), his bestselling blend of true crime and travelogue about Savannah, Georgia, that – by the author's own admission – was intended as beach-reading (Ricketson 1995). It is about actual people and events, though, and is written in a smooth narrative style befitting Berendt's years as an editor at *Esquire* magazine. In a three-sentence author's note, Berendt writes: 'Though this is a work of nonfiction, I have taken certain storytelling liberties, particularly having to do with the timing of events. Where the narrative strays from strict nonfiction, my intention has been to remain faithful to the characters and to the essential drift of events as they really happened' (1994: 389).

This note appears after the body of the book; in all likelihood, readers would not have seen it until after they finished the book and Berendt gives readers no specific information about the 'certain storytelling liberties' he takes. Later research by journalists and a journalism academic reveal a number of factual errors, some minor, others more important; there is some fabricated dialogue which Berendt terms 'rounding the corners to make a better narrative', an undisclosed contract with Jim Williams, who was charged and eventually cleared of murder, and accusations of Berendt using stories people told him without confirming details with others because they had the 'folkloric quality' he wanted for his book (Dufresne 1998: 78-79).

These matters go to the research and writing of Berendt's work, but the most serious problem in how Berendt establishes his relationship with readers is that he places a version of himself in the book four years before he actually arrives in Savannah. He describes himself witnessing an argument between Jim Williams, the main person in the book, and the young hustler who works for him, Danny Hansford. He describes himself attending the first two of the four trials of Williams for the murder of Hansford, and he describes himself at a midnight voodoo ritual with Williams from which the book's title emerges (ibid: 78). Bizarrely, and of most relevance here, Berendt devotes an entire chapter to describing a sexual encounter between Hansford and a young art student named Corinne who calls him a 'walking streak of sex' (Berendt 1994: 130). They have sex in the master-bedroom of Williams's mansion, and they have more sex in a graveyard where they are almost caught by passers-by; Corinne is impressed by Hansford's ability to maintain a 'rock-hard erection' throughout (ibid: 139). If that feels like too much information, consider Berendt's description of their first bout of sex:

> He put his arms around her and stroked her back with both hands, caressing her throat with both hands, caressing her throat lightly with kisses and sending a shiver down her spine. They tumbled onto the four-poster, and he began kissing her breasts

while at the same time pushing her skirt up and pulling down her panties. She reached down to remove her shoes, but before she could do it, he was pressing against her, probing with his fingers, gently and insistently. With the other hand he unzipped his fly. He took her buttocks tightly in his hands and pulled her toward him as he thrust into her. She breathed the salty smell of his T-shirt and felt his belt buckle rubbing against her stomach. Their rising body heat enclosed them like a steamy towel (ibid: 132).

Questioned about this, Berendt told me at the time the book was released that Corinne recounted the event in every particular (Ricketson 1995). Even down to the belt buckle rubbing on her stomach? Yes, he said. This strains credulity; pause for a moment and try imagining how that line of questioning went... Equally to the point, the chapter relies on one person's memory (Hansford was killed by the time Berendt arrived in Georgia); it places the reader literally in the bedroom, and it reads like pulp fiction.

The Scientific Approach to Bonking

Does this mean writing about sex and love-making is something that is, or should be, outside the boundaries of literary journalism? One way to smuggle the subject through customs (as it were) is to adopt a scientific approach, as Mary Roach does in her 2008 book, *Bonk: The Curious Coupling of Science and Sex*. A science journalist whose previous book was *Stiff: The Curious Lives of Human Cadavers* (2003), Roach seems intent on filling any gaps left after Woody Allen's 1972 film *Everything You Wanted to Know About Sex But were Afraid to Ask*. In one chapter about how the distance between a woman's vagina and her clitoris affects the ability to orgasm, Roach volunteers to be part of a scientific study about it. She finds herself using a mirror to see 'the real estate in question' because most men can better describe 'a woman's vulval particulars than can most women'. She recommends conducting this examination solo.

> Otherwise, you will run the risk of someone walking in on you and having to witness a scene that includes a mirror, the husband's Stanley Powerlock tape measure, and the half-undressed self, squatting. No one should have to see that. It's bad enough that you just had to read it. Also, put the tape measure away when you're done. My husband saw it on the bedside table and said: 'What are you measuring?' (Roach 2008: 70).

Roach's approach to writing about the science of sex satisfies our curiosity about the topic. It also offers the reader some distance on the topic – distance sweatily foreclosed by Berendt in his book. That Roach writes about sex humorously is doubly disarming; we smile as we read and we also identify with the embarrassment many feel about discussing details of sex and sexuality.

Conclusion: How to Write Well About Love-making

It may not be surprising, then, that a joint biography of the sex researchers, William Masters and Virginia Johnson, offers an example of how to write about sex and love-making. Thomas Maier's 2009 book, *Masters of Sex*, tells the story of the pioneering American researchers whose 1966 study *Human Sexual Response* draws on their personal observation and measuring of more than 10,000 orgasms by men and women in the United States in the 1950s and 1960s (Maier 2009: 172). Mrs Johnson, according to Maier, from a young age sexually adventurous, was in tune with her body and able to keep separate sexual pleasure and love:

> Virginia discovered the absence of devotion didn't mean she couldn't enjoy herself in the bedroom. Love wasn't necessary in reaching a physical climax, that intensity of feeling followed by a quiver of release. 'I never had any difficulty,' she said of orgasm. 'It was just more natural with some than with others. In fact, I didn't realise how wonderful some of the men were until they weren't in the picture' (Maier 2009: 18-19).

Mrs Johnson, a twice-divorced single mother of two children, became Masters' secretary and eventually his research assistant, because her warm candour and engaging manner put at ease the many prospective men and women needed for their study. Conversely, Masters was a brilliant, forward-thinking scientist but also taciturn and foreboding. But Maier also takes his biography into darker territory as he reveals how Masters exploited Johnson's economic vulnerability and virtually insisted she cooperate with him in conducting experiments using themselves as sexual partners. She complied, reflecting many years later that it might have been sexual harassment but she hadn't really thought of it that way at the time. As Maier writes:

> Forced into compliance by personal circumstances and the tenor of her times, Gini didn't act offended or recalcitrant in having sex with Bill. She accepted his overtures without complaint, part of a rationalization to herself. 'No – I was not comfortable with

it, particularly,' she insisted. 'I didn't want him at all, and had no interest in him. I don't know how to explain it' (Maier 2009: 129).

A television series of the same name (premièred on 29 September 2013), while beautifully made and brilliantly performed by Michael Sheen and Lizzy Caplan in the lead roles, was only loosely based on Maier's carefully researched work. It is certainly worth watching and includes a great deal more sex scenes than is common in period dramas of 1950s America, but for the purpose of this chapter the book is more important, at once informative, intimate, engaging and respectful. It offers at least a pathway for literary journalists to write about sex and love-making, though it can't and shouldn't be universalised as Maier's approach appears to be tied, quite appropriately, to his subject-matter.

References

Berendt, John (1994) *Midnight in the Garden of good and Evil*, New York: Vintage

Bowker, Gordon (2003) *Inside George Orwell*, London: Palgrave Macmillan

Conover, Ted (2000) *Newjack: Guarding Sing Sing*, New York: Random House

Dufresne, Marcel (1998) 'Why *Midnight* may be darker than you think', *Columbia Journalism Review*, May/June pp 78-79

Holden, Kate (2005) *In My Skin: A Memoir*, Melbourne: Text

Holden, Kate (2010) *The Romantic: Italian Nights and Days*, Melbourne: Text

Holmes, Richard (1995) Biography: Inventing the truth, Batchelor, John (ed.) *The Art of Literary Biography*, Oxford: Clarendon Press pp 15-25.

Jones, Glyn (ed.) (1989) *True Crime through History: True Stories of the 100 Most Infamous Murderers of the Last Two Centuries*, London: Magpie Books

Joseph, Sue (2016) *Behind the Text: Candid Conversations with Australian Creative nonfiction Writers*, Melbourne: Hybrid Publishers

Maier, Thomas (2009) *Masters of Sex: The Life and Times of William Masters and Virginia Johnson, the Couple Who Taught America How to Love*, New York: Basic Books

Milligan, Louise (2017) *Cardinal: The Rise and Fall of George Pell*, Carlton: Melbourne University Press

Orwell, George (1974 [1933]) *Down and Out in Paris and London*, Harmondsworth, Middlesex: Penguin

Preston, Richard (1994) *The Hot Zone*, New York: Doubleday

Ricketson, Matthew (1995) After midnight, *Herald Sun, Weekend*, 4 November p. 9

Ricketson, Matthew (2014) *Telling True Stories: Navigating the Challenges of Writing Narrative Non-fiction*, Sydney: Allen & Unwin

Roach, Mary (2008) *Bonk: The Curious Coupling of Science and Sex*, New York: W. W. Norton

Sims, Norman and Kramer, Mark (1995) *Literary Journalism: A New Collection of the Best American Nonfiction*, New York: Ballantine

Steinem, Gloria (1983) I was a Playboy bunny, *Outrageous Acts and Everyday Rebellions*, New York: Holt, Rinehart and Winston pp 29-69

Talese, Gay (2016) *The Voyeur's Motel*, London: Grove Press

Taylor, D. J. (2003) *Orwell: The Life*, London: Vintage

Wheelwright, Julie (2017) The orgy next door: An exploration of ethical relationships in Gay Talese's *Thy Neighbor's Wife* and *The Voyeur's Motel*, *Literary Journalism Studies*, Fall, Vol. 9, No. 2 pp 28-50. Available online at https://ialjs.org/wpcontent/uploads/2017/11/02-Orgy-28-51.pdf

Note on the Author

Matthew Ricketson is an academic and journalist. He is Professor of Communication at Deakin University and has worked as a journalist at the *Age*, the *Australian* and *Time Australia* magazine. He is the author of three books and editor of two. In 2011 he was appointed by the federal government to work with Ray Finkelstein QC on an Inquiry into the Media and Media Regulation which reported in 2012.

Chapter 3

'I am that girl': How the Saxon Mullins Account Disrupted Consent Laws in New South Wales

As a survivor of sexual assault, Saxon Mullins's right to anonymity is, by law, set in stone. But, on 6 May 2018, she decided to go public. Sue Joseph analyses the broadcast which led to the New South Wales Attorney General referring the state's consent laws to the NSW Law Reform Commission.

> *Enthusiastic consent is really easy to determine ... if it's not an enthusiastic 'yes', then it's not enough. If it's not an enthusiastic 'yes', it's a 'no'.*
> *That's it. And then, you're committing a crime.*
> Saxon Mullins, in 'I am that girl', ABC, 2018

Introduction

As a survivor of sexual assault, Saxon Mullins's right to anonymity is, by Australian law, set in stone. So it was a riveting moment on 6 May 2018 to wake up in Australia to her face and her voice, telling her story in her own words. More than 24 hours before *Four Corners* went to air, social media exploded with excerpts on Facebook and Twitter retagged and resent as the day went on. The story was also picked up by Reddit. By 8.30pm the following evening, 785,000 viewers tuned in to the national broadcaster to watch the long-form current affairs broadcast entitled 'I am that girl'. The programme was tagged 'The case that put sexual consent on trial' – and it did. According to Cathy Camera: 'As Saxon Mullins bravely told her rape story on *Four Corners*, Twitter lit up in horror and disbelief' (Camera 2018). The following morning after airing, the New South Wales government referred the state's consent laws to the Law Reform Commission.

Goddard et al. discuss the current affairs genre within television. They say it is a programme category 'where television's powers of popular engagement and visual impact intersect most directly with its functions as a provider of knowledge and as a major "forum" of the public sphere' (2001: 74). As such, *Four Corners* – Australia's leading and longest-running investigative journalism and current affairs programme – prides itself on its public engagement. When it entered its 50th year of broadcast back in 2011, Mark Scott, managing director of the ABC at the time, said:

> Four half a century *Four Corners* has been giving us the kind of stories through which we could take the pulse of Australian life. ... In 2011, as in 1961, it still gives ... us the kind of stories ... that awaken public interest and bring about change in ourselves and our opinions that ultimately lead to lasting change in public policy and the law (Scott 2011).

Indeed, Mullins shared her story with Four Corners 'in the hope it will provoke a discussion about consent' (Mullins, in Milligan and Carter 2018). Response was immediate: Four Corners and Saxon Mullins set the scene for a far-reaching debate about consent laws in Australia.

The case

Saxon Mullins was an 18-year-old virgin at the time of the sexual assault during a night out (12 May 2013) in Kings Cross, Sydney, with her best friend Brittany Watts. They were drinking and Mullins admits she drank too much. By 4am, Mullins and Watts were dancing in well-known nightclub Soho, owned by Andrew Lazarus at the time (it was to close down in June 2015). A young man started dancing with Mullins; he was the 21-year-old son of Lazarus, Luke Lazarus. He told her he was part-owner of the club and offered to take her to the VIP section. She agreed and followed him. They are caught on CCTV at 4.02am, Lazarus leading her through an exit door to an outside lane. Mullins is seen pointing backwards up the stairs.

Hourigan Lane runs behind the club. It was here where Lazarus – ten minutes after meeting Mullins on the dance-floor – sexually assaulted her. In 2015, Luke Lazarus, after a jury trial found him guilty of the sexual assault of Saxon Mullins, was sentenced to five years' jail, with a three-year, non-parole period. Lazarus was incarcerated for 11 months before his appeal was heard in May 2017, when his conviction was quashed by Judge Robyn Tupman. Tupman believed Mullins did *not* consent but that Lazarus did *not* know that. She acquitted Lazarus.

The NSW Court of Criminal Appeal in Sydney later that year in November, in a second appeal submitted by the Crown, found that Judge Tupman erred in her findings 'by failing to state in her judgement what steps Lazarus took to determine whether Saxon was consenting, as required under the law' (Milligan 2018). But it also decided that Lazarus would not be re-tried saying it 'was not in the interests of justice' (ibid).

Text analysis – long-form broadcast journalism

'I am that girl', presented by reporter Louise Milligan, ran for 45 minutes on the night of 7 May 2018. In the 24 hours before the programme went to air, it was accompanied by teasers on Facebook and Twitter, with accounts run by the ABC and Fairfax. There is also a long-form digital version of the programme written by Louise Milligan, uploaded in the early hours of the day of the broadcast. The following analysis focuses on the long-form broadcast.

The programme initially tells the story from the point of view of Saxon Mullins before recounting, through the court transcript, Luke Lazarus's version of the night; and then we hear from experts Professor Annie Cossins, University of NSW, Dr Ellie Freedman, the medical director of the Northern Sydney Sexual Assault Service and Stephen Odgers, the Chair of the Criminal Law Committee of the NSW Bar Association. It demonstrates the hallmarks of documentary reporting: scene re-creation, dialogue, the use of voice-over, face-to-face, in-depth interviewing, balance, personalised film-making and the drawing on expert voices. The programme tackles the subject chronologically and attempts to achieve 'balance', even though the Lazarus family did not agree to take part. Transcripts from the trial and appeal of Luke Lazarus are used instead of him appearing in person.

It opens with a night-time sequence shot of Saxon Mullins walking through the streets of Kings Cross and she comments: 'I never knew what panic attacks felt like until my incident. I never knew what it felt like to be utterly helpless' ('I am that girl' 2018). Next Mullins, directly to camera, says: 'My name is Saxon Mullins. In 2013, when I was 18-years-old, I was raped in an alleyway in Kings Cross.' This is powerful in its simplicity. Her voice is strong and her eyes clear. The programme continues, setting the scene with electronic music and a collage of moving shots of night life in Kings Cross.

Four Corners is known for its sparse studio set – the subject sitting in front of a black back-drop so there are no distractions, either speaking across the screen to the interviewer, off-camera, or addressing the audience through piece-to-camera technique, with the viewer invited to focus on the person speaking. Reporter Milligan explains and contextualises the story: 'In May 2013, two 18-year-olds caught a train from the NSW Central Coast to Sydney's Kings Cross looking forward to their first big night out in the city.' Through re-enactments and CCTV footage, the story continues, set against dance music and fade-in and -out shots of different nightclub spots in the Cross. CCTV footage shows Mullins and her best friend Brittany Watts entering Soho nightclub just before 4am. It is here that Mullins meets Luke Lazarus. They are caught on CCTV leaving the club through a back exit into Hourigan Lane. Mullins is seen gesturing back up the stairs. The last thing the CCTV shows is Luke Lazarus taking Mullins by the hand and leading her out the rear exit into the lane, ten minutes after they meet on the dance-floor.

The grimness of a dark alleyway in Kings Cross in the middle of the night is captured. There are close-ups of the gutter and the wall, and leaves on the ground. As Robert Drew explains (2001): 'What the prime-time documentary adds to the journalistic spectrum is the ability to let viewers experience the sense of being somewhere else, drawing them into dramatic developments in the lives of people caught up in stories of importance.' *Four Corners* manages these techniques effectively: dark shots, for instance, conjure a sense of foreboding. Next, according to Mullins, she told Lazarus she wanted to go back to her friend; when he pulled her stockings and underwear down, she pulled them back up; and when she turned to leave, he pulled her back. It was at this point Mullins says he told her to 'put your fucking hands on the wall' ('I am that girl' 2018).

She did as she was told. She says: 'It was a demand. From someone I had never met before. In a dark alleyway. Alone. And I was scared.' A re-enactment shows extreme close-ups of shadows, spider-webs and the fence. There are two hands seen against the fence. We see what Mullins would have seen during the attack. At this point of her story, the close-up of Mullins talking to Milligan shows distress; she struggles to recover. She looks away and is clearly suffering. Milligan does not interrupt but waits for her to tell her story, in her own way. The music stops and there is a slight delay as Mullins tries to find the words – her emotional distress is clear. She tells Milligan in an extreme close-up: 'And ... And that's kind of when, he ah, um, I don't know how to say that bit, I umm ... He ah, he had anal sex with me.' Milligan asks: 'And you had never had any sex before?' Mullins shakes her head and (in close-up) whispers: 'No ... It was pretty painful. And um, I just kind of froze, you know? ... Like just wait 'til it was over' ('I am that girl' 2018).

Milligan, in voice-over, says Saxon Mullins says she told Luke Lazarus to stop. We then go back to the studio. Milligan asks Mullins: 'And what did he do when you told him to stop?' Mullins replies: 'Nothing.' Milligan follows up with a leading question: 'Would you ever have wanted your first sexual experience to be on your knees in the gravel, anal sex?' Mullins: '... I didn't even get kissed until I was 17-years-old. I had this grandiose ... romantic – it'll be by candlelight on a bed of roses; with someone who loves me.' She then looks straight at Milligan and says, emphatically and in close-up: '... you know, no-one dreams of their first time being in an alleyway with someone whose name they can't even remember. No-one wants that' ('I am that girl' 2018). Milligan then switches to highlighting Luke Lazarus's behaviour the day after the assault. Accompanied by tracking shots down the main street of Kings Cross, text message bubbles appear and are read in voice-over by two male actors:

> LUKE LAZARUS: I honestly have zero recollection of calling you, was a sick night. Took a chick's virginity, lol.
>
> FRIEND: Bahahaha. Nice popping cherries. Tight?
>
> LUKE LAZARUS: So tight. It's a pretty gross story. Tell ya later ('I am that girl' 2018).

Immediate cutaway back to Mullins in the studio. She tries to explain her week following the assault. She becomes emotional: 'I took a week off work. I sat in the bath. I didn't want to see anyone. I was so humiliated. I didn't want to do anything. I just wanted to sleep' ('I am that girl' 2018).

With more shots of Kings Cross, including the famous Coca Cola sign, archived footage of newsreader Hugh Riminton is used: 'The son of a wealthy Sydney businessman is facing fourteen years jail for a sexual assault outside a Kings Cross nightclub part-owned by his father.' Milligan spells out what is needed for a conviction in NSW. She says, back-dropped with archived footage of Lazarus arriving and leaving the Downing Centre courthouse in Sydney: 'The prosecution had to prove three things: that Luke Lazarus and Saxon Mullins had sex, that Saxon was not consenting and that Luke Lazarus knew that or didn't care.' We hear Luke Lazarus's defence from the transcript of his first trial when he pleaded not guilty. Voiced by an actor and backed by still photographs of Luke Lazarus and thumping techno music, against the same tracking shots of the back alley and re-enactment of a couple there, we hear Lazarus's version of events: 'What happened on the night between Saxon and I, I honest to God believed, was consensual' ('I am that girl' 2018). CCTV footage is repeated, showing Lazarus leading Mullins out into the laneway; we hear Lazarus's court testimony and an apology to Saxon Mullins. He was sentenced to a minimum of three years' jail, with no parole. When Milligan asks Mullins what her reaction was to the verdict, we have a close-up of her, choosing her words carefully, her distress palpable: 'It's pretty complex. There's a bit of relief. Not only for, it's over, but they believed me. And then there's the inevitable bit of guilt. I can't help but feel I destroyed someone's life' ('I am that girl' 2018).

As mentioned above, Lazarus appealed against his sentence and won. That appeal was then overturned later in 2017, but it was decided at that point that there would not be a re-trial. There is archived footage of Lazarus leaving the Appeals Court. Milligan asks Mullins how she felt after the final appeal: 'I guess it's just this instant feeling of deflated. That was it. That was all we had and they, two seconds, just went, no. It's over' ('I am that girl' 2018). At the end, there is a close-up of Mullins talking to Milligan; she is emphatic:

> ... I think we need to teach people about making sure that the person that you are with wants to be with you. Enthusiastic consent is really easy to determine. And I think if you don't have that, then you're not good to go. All you need to say is: 'Do you want to be here?' And very clearly: 'Do you want to have sex with me? Do you want to be doing what we're doing?' And if it's not an enthusiastic yes, then it's not enough. If it's not an enthusiastic yes, it's a no. That's it. And then, you're committing a crime. Simple as that ('I am that girl' 2018).

Metrics

Interestingly, 785,000 viewers across the country watched *Four Corners* on the night which is 11 per cent below the series average for 2018; but a further 38,000 watched it on the ABC's iview (45 per cent *more* than series average for 2018). The feature article by Milligan the morning of the broadcast was shared broadly on social media by influencers, journalists and organisations. The video posted the day before the programme went to air had: 80,000 views on Facebook, reached 162,000 people, generated 2,500 comments/reactions and 400 shares. The second video posted the morning of broadcast had 104,000 views, 250,000 reach, 1,630 comments/reactions and 200 shares. The videos posted on Twitter were viewed close to 40,000 times. Across three days – before, during and after broadcast – the *Four Corners'* Twitter account generated well over 200,000 impressions and #4Corners trended on the Monday and Tuesday (author correspondence with Executive Producer of *Four Corners*, Sally Neighbour, 9 April 2019). But it was the online feature by Louise Milligan that proved the most successful in terms of reach. Produced by the *Four Corners'* digital team, it was the best performing article for the year, with more than 540,000 views.

Conclusion

The effectiveness of the *Four Corners* format is that the audience is given access, albeit guided by the reporter, to the people involved. We watch Saxon Mullins discuss her experience. We see her attempt to control her emotions; we see true consequences of trauma on her face and in the way she holds her body. We even get to hear her empathic response to sending another young person to jail.

Nine months after the programme was aired, Saxon Mullins was awarded the Young People's Human Rights Award by the Australian Human Rights Commission. According to the judging panel:

> ... Saxon exhibited immense bravery in publicly sharing her story of sexual assault in order to promote debate around the need for legal reforms. Her advocacy triggered a review into NSW sexual assault laws to better protect victims and survivors of sexual assault and violence (Australian Humans Rights Commission 2018).

As Drew concludes (2001): 'The right kind of documentary programming should raise more interest than it can satisfy, more questions than it should try to answer.'

References

ABC News (2018) NSW government directs Law Reform Commission to review consent laws, 8 May. Available online at https://www.abc.net.au/news/2018-05-08/law-reform-commission-to-review-consent-laws/9738402, accessed on 1 March 2019

Australian Humans Rights Commission (2018) Winners announced – 2018 Human Rights Awards, 14 December. Available online at https://www.humanrights.gov.au/news/stories/winners-announced-2018-human-rights-awards, accessed on 2 April 2019

Camera, Cathy (2018) Sex without consent is rape. Courts around the world must catch up, *Guardian*, 9 May. Available online at https://www.theguardian.com/commentisfree/2018/may/09/sex-without-consent-is-courts-around-the-world-must-catch-up, accessed on 11 April 2019

Drew, Robert (2001) A Nieman year spent pondering, *Nieman Reports*, Fall, 15 September. Available online at https://niemanreports.org/articles/a-nieman-year-spent-pondering-storytelling/, accessed on 2 April 2019

Goddard, Peter, Corner, John and Richardson, Kay (2001) The formation of *World in Action*: A case study in the history of current affairs journalism, *Journalism*, Vol. 2, No.1 pp 73-90

'I am that girl' (2018) *Four Corners*, ABC, 7 May. Available online at https://www.abc.net.au/4corners/i-am-that-girl/9736126, accessed on 7 May 2018

Milligan, Louise (2018) 'I am that girl', ABC, 7 May. Available online at https://www.abc.net.au/news/2018-05-07/kings-cross-rape-case-that-put-consent-on-trial/9695858, accessed on 1 March 2019

Milligan, Louise and Carter, Lucy (2018) NSW Attorney General calls for review of sexual consent laws following *Four Corners* program, *ABC News*. Available online at https://www.abc.net.au/news/2018-05-08/nsw-attorney-general-calls-for-review-of-sexual-consent-laws/9734988, accessed on 1 March 2019

Scott, Mark (2011) Fifty years of *Four Corners*, 22 August. Viewed on 1 March 2019 at https://www.abc.net.au/4corners/fifty-years-of-four-corners/2847348

Chapter 4

Sluts and Sex Objects: Memoir and the Millennial Journalist

Kylie Cardell and Emma Maguire examine the writings of Karley Sciortino and Jessica Valenti who dare to appropriate normally pejorative terms such as 'slut' and 'sex object' in order to promote progressive notions about gender and sexuality.

Introduction

Karley Sciortino and Jessica Valenti write about sex. In a range of media, on websites, for print and digital magazines and newspapers, in podcasts, books and documentaries, Sciortino and Valenti use both reportage and personal experience as example and argument in framing a sex-positive, education-focused and feminist-aligned discourse that seeks to explore dominant cultural understandings of sex in the contemporary world. These writers are young, political, self-consciously and self-righteously Millennial and they are professional journalists at a time of rapid change for the profession.

Rosalind Coward (2013) writes about the increasing pressure on journalists to 'speak personally' within their professional mandate; as sex writers, Sciortino and Valenti already negotiate with this imperative in particular and significant ways. Writing about sex, gender and feminism, Sciortino and Valenti occupy a particularly fraught nexus for the journalist, one necessarily located in-between or at the cusp of public and private, professional and personal worlds, and one that mobilises public appeal for confessional narratives to make political interventions. Sciortino and Valenti use journalism to construct themselves, and young women like them, as sexual subjects rather than sexual objects. But the legacy of post-feminism and the patriarchal tenets embedded in discourses of sexual revolution mean that it is not always clear where buying into sexual objectification ends and claiming one's sexuality begins for young women.

This chapter discusses two recent publications: *Vice.com* journalist, *Vogue* columnist and sex-positive educator Sciortino's 2018 collection of essays *Slutever: Dispatches from a Sexually Autonomous Woman in a Post-Shame World;* and feminist blogger and *Guardian* columnist Valenti's 2016 *Sex Object: A Memoir.* These texts are timely examples of how contemporary female journalists negotiate and deploy life narrative in the context of their professional work.

In memoirs published concurrently to journalistic work produced elsewhere, these writers take up a potential of the memoir genre, as Gillian Whitlock (2007: 135) observes, to 'supplement' what has been 'edited out of preceding genres of report'. Whitlock is discussing the appeal of the embedded journalist memoir, a subgenre that gained popular traction during the successive US Iraqi conflicts of the 1990s, but the mode resonates beyond this location or context. For Whitlock, it is clear that the war reporter uses memoir to speak 'more personally' than they, ostensibly, have previously been allowed; they use it to confess, to testify and to frame an individual ethical response to an experience they have also traded on for profit (ibid: 134). In contrast, Sciortino and Valenti use their life writing to defend and contextualise the personal experience that audiences already perceive as indistinguishable from their copy: the work of memoir here is to re-route and re-circuit various ascriptions of identity that they both negotiate and deploy in their professional persona.

Sciortino: The Empowered Slut

In the opening essay of *Slutever: Dispatches from a Sexually Autonomous Woman in a Post-Shame World* (2018), a chapter titled 'Manifesto', Sciortino sets out her terms of reference. While the word 'slut' is usually understood as pejorative, Sciortino asserts it is in fact also 'great' (ibid: 1) because it describes an identity that allows women to pursue and enjoy their sexual desires without 'moral obstacle' (ibid: 2). This is 'lucky' because 'it's pretty safe to say that every woman will be called a slut at least once in her lifetime. I, personally, have the distinct pleasure of being called a slut at least twelve times a day – just one of the many perks of being a sex writer in the age of internet trolls (*hair flip*)' (ibid: 1). Sciortino's description here makes clear that even though she has reclaimed the word slut, crafting a public identity around her sex life makes her a target for abuse. Which is why, she notes: 'While many women today are vocally anti-slut shaming, very few women are openly slutty' (ibid: 5). Sciortino's humorous, ironic, autobiographical voice almost masks the fact that performing nonchalance (*hair flip*) about the abuse volleyed at her on a daily basis is a vital survival strategy that enables her to continue to work under conditions that would be unacceptable in most contemporary workplaces. Sciortino's 'dispatches' from the front lines of sex and sex-positive cultures illuminate the challenges she faces in owning a slutty identity, and she models resilience and irreverence as strategies for progressing female sexual autonomy.

Sciortino's wry, cynical persona and performative gestural narration deploys another identity she also claims quite overtly throughout the memoir: that of the Millennial. Sciortino is a Millennial subject and *Slutever* is an exploration of 'post-woke social-justice Millennial whatever' (ibid: 11). The problem driving Sciortino's discussion is articulated as a uniquely contemporary one: 'To be a slut or not to be a slut? That is the modern feminist question' (ibid: 5), but, like the Shakespearean allusion in her phrasing, the dichotomy underlying this question is recursively familiar.

It is worth noting that Sciortino is not the only Millennial to take up 'slut' as a label and subject position from which to 'report back' on slutty living in a normative culture. Performance artist and adult model Madison Young (2014), in her memoir *Daddy*, describes the joy of taking up the identity of the slut:

> *Slut.* It conjured an image of being ravaged and undone. It brought about a sense of calm and well-being; it validated my sexual self. … it was sensuous, exciting, and full of life. Sluts deserve to be worshipped and adored, and at the same time to give themselves to others. Sluts filled chalices with their come, sweat, and blood; sluts blessed the town. I was empowered by my slut self… (ibid: 176, emphasis in original).

Here, Young describes the slut as a quasi-spiritual figure. At once sacrificial and godlike, empowered and undone, with the ability both to soothe and excite, the slut lives to serve and commands others to serve her. She sounds, in Young's rendering, almost saintly. The slut has always been a figure plagued by contradictory demands. One example is the paradox of youthful feminine sexuality: if girls do not 'put out' they are labelled prudes, but if they do, they risk being labelled a slut. Another example, and one that goes to the heart of the figure of the slut, is the sexual double-standard which celebrates promiscuous men but condemns promiscuous women. Here, however, the contradictions that historically entrap the figure of the slut are used to elevate her. She is dexterous enough to slide along any continuum. The spiritual imagery works in a similar way: once trapped within the Madonna/whore dualism, the slut here 'deserves' worship rather than denigration. The whore now has the power to bless and to command adoration as an object of worship.

But what does the celebration of the slut as progressive feminist identity highlight about contemporary sex journalism? Sciortino describes the slut as both an aspirational mode of feminine sexual empowerment and brings in her own lived experience as an illustrative tool. In Sciortino's manifesto, the slut is described as having a curious mind, an adventurous spirit and a lust for exploration (ibid: 8-9). This is fitting because imagining a mode of feminine sexuality that breaks free from the bonds of the sexual double-standard is, indeed, ground-breaking work.

But despite this positive image Sciortino creates for the slut, she concedes that life as a slut is difficult in a 'sex-negative society' (ibid: 7). The book goes on to describe experiences of being ostracised and slut-shamed by teenage peers, being shamed and dumped by romantic partners, having to negotiate a fractured relationship with her mother who did not understand Sciortino's lifestyle, and getting caught in an existential crisis about what her future looks like given there are few social scripts that end well for sluts. There are also instances of violence, manipulation and emotional confusion that Sciortino experiences in the course of her slutty experiences. So although the title of the book mentions a 'post-shame world', Sciortino's reports from the front line of sex-positivity reveal a culture that remains deeply ambivalent if not outright hostile to sexually empowered women, a phenomenon she optimistically refers to as 'growing pains' (ibid: 5).

Far from undermining Sciortino's claims about the revolutionary power of the slut, though, these examples make visible the hard work required by arbiters of cultural change. As a woman journalist writing autobiographically about sex in a culture that is deeply anxious about women's sexual agency, Sciortino's 'dispatches' do important work in modelling sex-positive feminism.

Valenti and Confessional Memoir

Jessica Valenti, too, pays careful attention to the power of language and the politics of naming in her memoir, *Sex Object* (2016): 'This book is called *Sex Object* not because I relish the idea of identifying as such: I don't do it coyly or to flatter myself. I don't use the term because I think I'm particularly sexy or desirable, though I've been called both those things before at opportune moments' (ibid: 2). Like Sciortino, Valenti addresses the way in which language is used to diminish or contain women's public selves by braiding feminine sexuality and shame. Where Sciortino uses her journalism to investigate and educate about sexual culture, Valenti, too, deploys her personal sexual experience as a way of breaking taboos and silence around women's sex lives.

But Valenti's tone is less flippant when addressing the kinds of abuse and censure that follow women who dare to explore such topics in public, and her writing acts as testimony to the ways in which sexual objectification disempowers women who take up public space. In 'Subways', one of Valenti's most devastating essays, she recounts her (many, accumulated) experiences of being subjected to indecent exposure on the New York underground. Valenti's narrative 'I' in this essay tellingly shifts between first-person singular and plural: as a teenager, Valenti learns to avoid 'the two worst times for dicks on subways: when the train car is empty or when it's crowded ... if I found myself in an empty car, I would immediately leave – even if it meant changing cars as the train moved, which terrified me' (ibid: 57). By the essay's close, Valenti concludes: 'The message is clear: we are here for their enjoyment and little else. We have to walk through the rest of the day knowing that our discomfort gave someone else a hard-on' (ibid: 65). While feminists have historically fought for women's access and rights to public space and voice, Valenti testifies to a dark reality. For women in these experiences, what it means is 'that public spaces are not really public for you, but a series of private moments that you can't prevent or erase' (ibid: 65).

Throughout her memoir, Valenti is acute and devastating on the ways in which 'public' is not necessarily a safer space for women who already suffer statistically and disproportionately from the effects of violence and domestic abuse in the private sphere. In *Sex Object*, Valenti turns to a different public, the cultural and digital space that she occupies as a journalist writing about sex and gender, but one that she similarly reveals as complex and as brutal as a New York subway. The final chapter of the memoir is titled 'Endnotes (2008-2015)' and it reproduces, without comment, some of the extremely abusive emails and threatening or insulting social media posts Valenti has received. For ten pages, the reader is confronted with a barrage of messages complaining of Valenti's various uglinesses, calling her a 'cunt' and telling her she needs to be 'gagged and burned alive'; one of the entries consists only of the words 'fuck you' repeated without break or punctuation for two pages (ibid: 194-196). It amounts to only a tiny sampling of the abuse that Valenti and other women receive online daily (Mantilla 2013: 566).

While Valenti shows sexual violence is pervasive even for women who do not take up public voices, her work as a journalist who uses personal and confessional modes to write about sex has particular implications here. In 'Authenticity, confession, and female sexuality: From Bridget to Bitchy', Fiona Handyside (2012: 44) explores a 'continuum' of 'the fictional and the factual' that exists in first-person narration of sexual experience. While Bridget Jones, the protagonist of Helen Fielding's diary novel, adopts a distinctive, self-deprecating narrative voice, the anonymous blogger behind the ironically inter-referential *Bitchy Jones's Diary* deploys conventions of the 'confessional' to secure her audience's trust and confidence. Far from compromising an audience's sense of 'truthfulness', adopting a pseudonym can encourage 'the impression that there will be *greater* self-exposure, that a real identity needs to be protected, and the reader is, therefore, simultaneously courted (offered the possibility of access to "a secret truth") and held at a distance (not given the detail of a real-life name)' (ibid: 44). Yet while that practice of using pseudonyms works to market sex writing as authentic, it also bolsters the idea that the author requires protection. Both Valenti and Sciortino represent a departure from this tradition: Valenti, in her memoir, makes a point of being public, of attaching both a name and life to the narration of her gendered experience, but she also shows the consequences of this visibility for women journalists in particular.

Conclusions

In a discussion of contemporary women's erotic memoirs, Joel Gwynne (2013: 21) observes: 'Narratives of female promiscuity are relegated to the private sphere largely due to limited public space for their expression, despite the fact that the twenty-first century bears witness to a diverse and increasing range of sexual economies and practices represented in the mainstream media.' The erotic memoirs that Gwynne discusses are presented as memoir in a classic sense; the author is narrating a set of experiences connected thematically as the lived reality of the author. Gwynne finds a set of texts that, while apparently transgressive in that they narrate and present highly graphic sexual encounters from a feminine viewpoint, 'remain trapped within male-dominated discourses that are limiting to women's empowerment' (ibid: 23). Correspondingly, Gwynne frames these erotic memoirs as pornography, using both feminist theory and media taxonomy to read and discuss particular features and tropes. The memoirs that Gwynne reads narrate and market private sexual experience and appeal to an audience invested in transgressive and confessional autobiographical discourse. In the case of women who write about sex, however, where a professional identity as a journalist underwrites the narration, the contract and deployment of the writer's position as a confessing sexual subject is different in crucial ways. That is, while Sciortino and Valenti reveal intimate and erotic detail in their memoirs, these texts are neither strategically marketed as nor correspond in their narrative arc and depictions to erotica or pornography in the way the memoirs Gwynne discusses do. Instead, Sciortino and Valenti choose to deploy intimate detail and explicit narration of 'private' experience but in a context, both paratextual and narrated, that must be read in relation to their status as journalists. That is, they are using their lived experience and their own confessional voices to make the broader power dynamics of contemporary sexuality both public and political and, in doing so, to reveal the stakes and the stakeholders embattled in the fight to police women's ownership of their sexuality.

Both Sciortino and Valenti develop journalistic personas, allowing them to navigate the conflicted territory of writing personally about sex and gender. Specifically, Sciortino claims the label slut, formulated by the bringing together of sex-positivity and feminism not only as theoretical positions but as a lifestyle. By modelling the contemporary slut – who is free to enjoy multiple partners and a variety of sexual tastes and is accepting of others who do the same – Sciortino's writing both illuminates radical potential and suggests strategies of irony and optimism to negotiate its limitations. Thus, Sciortino leans in to a post-feminist discourse which tends to assume that the power of equality is available for the sexual feminine subject to grasp, if she would only reach for it. In contrast, Valenti's adaptation of the label 'sex object' demonstrates a striving for empowerment against an incredibly powerful and prevalent patriarchal culture. The tone in which she ends the book – not with her own voice, but with the voices of 'gendertrolls' (Mantilla op cit) – construes a sense of crushing despair and eliminates the possibility of a happy ending for the sluts and sex objects of the world. However, this despair is incomplete and, in fact, demonstrates the need for the fight in which both Valenti and Sciortino are engaged.

Both Valenti and Sciortino powerfully subvert the gaze which they are subject to in publicly claiming an open and strident feminine sexuality. It is a difficult line that these writers walk between using the misogynistic appeal of labels like slut and sex object to market their work as journalists, and using these labels to critique and undermine a sexist culture that punishes women for their sexuality. In effect, Valenti and Sciortino demand to have it both ways – to sell themselves as sex objects and use this marketability professionally to critique dominant power structures. This tension begs us to ask whether, ultimately, trading on these labels is buying into a cultural agreement about the oppression at the root of this language. Maybe it is, but it is also why we must listen to these writers who are challenging so bravely the public discourses that oppress and shame feminine sexuality.

References

Coward, Rosalind (2013) *Speaking Personally: The Rise of Subjective and Confessional Journalism*, Basingstoke: Palgrave Macmillan

Gwynne, Joel (2013) *Erotic Memoirs and Postfeminism: The Politics of Pleasure*, Basingstoke: Palgrave Macmillan

Handyside, Fiona (2012) Authenticity, confession and female sexuality: From Bridget to Bitchy, *Psychology & Sexuality*, Vol. 3, No. 1 pp 41-53

Mantilla, Karla (2013) Gendertrolling: Misogyny adapts to new media, *Feminist Studies*, Vol. 39, No. 2 pp 563-570

Sciortino, Karley (2018) *Slutever: Dispatches from a Sexually Autonomous Woman in a Post-Shame World*, New York and Boston: Grand Central Publishing

Valenti, Jessica (2016) *Sex Object: A Memoir*, New York: HarperCollins

Whitlock, Gillian (2007) *Soft Weapons: Autobiography in Transit*, Chicago: University of Chicago Press

Note on the Authors

Dr Kylie Cardell is a Senior Lecturer in English at Flinders University, South Australia. She is the author of *Dear World: Contemporary Uses of the Diary* (2014) and editor (with Kate Douglas) of *Telling Tales: Autobiographies of Childhood and Youth* (2015). Kylie is an executive member for the International Auto/Biography Association (IABA) Asia-Pacific and co-directs the Flinders Life Narrative Research Group (Flinders University). She is the essays editor for the scholarly Australian journal *Life Writing*.

Dr Emma Maguire is a lecturer in English and Writing at James Cook University. She researches girlhood, digital media and life writing. Her book *Girls, Autobiography, Media: Gender and Self-Mediation in Digital Economies* (2018) is out now with Palgrave Macmillan.

Chapter 5

She Will Not Be Silenced: Lydia Cacho and the Terrible Dangers of Covering International Sex Trafficking

Lydia Cacho has spent her entire career investigating the ways social, political and economic systems create, perpetuate and benefit from the international sex market – and she has done so at great personal cost. Todd Schack outlines her unique reporting style – and suggests she offers a model from which journalism students can learn so much.

According to the International Labour Organisation (ILO), there has never before been more slaves than are alive today. Throughout the five-year period 2012-2017, 89 million people experienced some form of slavery and, of those, 43 per cent were bought and sold into international markets for sex, amounting to 38 million sex slaves around the world (ILO 2017).

Most journalism ignores or marginalises the topic. Yet, as the celebrated journalist and investigator of mafias and markets, Roberto Saviano, puts it, the issue of international sex trafficking is 'the Lydia Cacho cause' (2012; see also Vulliamy 2015). Indeed, Lydia Cacho has spent an entire career investigating the ways in which our current social, political and economic systems have created, perpetuated and benefited from the international sex market – and she has done so at great personal cost. She lives under continuous threat of death and has been kidnapped, tortured and threatened with rape in attempts to silence her (see Cacho 2012). But Lydia Cacho will not be intimidated.

In *Slavery Inc.: The Untold Story of International Sex Trafficking* (2012), she provides, in effect, a 'how-to' guide for covering the commodification of women and girls as sex slaves as an activist journalist. It is the purpose of this chapter to detail how Cacho's work digs to the root causes of this issue, how she exposes the economic imperatives at the heart of the market and how so-called modern, Western, liberal, even feminist notions of sexuality serve to perpetuate the international sex slavery market.

The Lydia Cacho Model
Blending First-Person Narratives with Investigative Reporting

Regarding her writing and her method, Cacho hints that, early on, she was influenced by a group of extraordinary writers, some investigative, some literary and all famous for their immersive reporting and ability to uncover deep socio-political truths. She writes about her early career, stating that: 'Back then I went to Mexico City to buy books – the entire collection of Ryszard Kapuscinski, everything written by Eduardo Galeano, Truman Capote, Joan Didion, Tom Wolfe and ... Günter Wallraff' (Cacho 2016: 22).

This list of writers makes perfect sense considering Cacho's writing and method, particularly in her book, *Slavery, Inc.*, which is a blend of first-person narratives, investigative reporting and research, and also what can properly be called 'slave testimonials'. First, she draws the reader in with first-person narratives of her attempts to get the story of international sex trafficking by going undercover, some of which reads like adventure fiction. She was not only inspired but mentored by Günther Wallraff, writing of him that the German journalist would '... later became a friend and an advisor when I began investigating mafias' (ibid: 23). She also discusses doing so with Antonio Salas who uncovered an international sex slavery market using disguise and a hidden camera for his book *The Year I Trafficked Women* (2004).

For her book, *Slavery, Inc.*, she also goes undercover, as a wealthy high-roller interested in buying male prostitutes in Cambodia, as a tourist in Burma and as a nun in Mexico, visiting the notorious La Merced neighbourhood in Mexico City. Years earlier, in 2004, she published a book, *The Demons of Eden*, which uncovers an international child pornography ring, unmasking the powerful Mexican businessmen and government officials who work to protect it. The book launch itself was held under armed guard. As a result of this book, however, and despite being given four armed bodyguards by the Mexican government for 24-hour protection, in 2005 she was kidnapped, beaten, tortured and threatened with rape.

It later emerged that the kidnapping had been organised by various local, state and federal police departments, at least five state governors and many highly respected businessmen. Due to an extraordinary set of circumstances she was freed – only to be charged with libel against the very businessman who was on video talking about the girls he had had kidnapped, tortured and raped. But none of this stopped her. She continued writing and launched the investigation that became *Slavery, Inc.* In one passage from this book, she writes of being at a restaurant with friends, when she is approached by a powerful *mafioso* of Los Zetas drug cartel:

> 'Look, Ms Cacho, you are the bravest woman in this country and I want you to know that we have more in common than you may think. ... If you allow me, I'll eliminate the precious governor and Nacif. We have to clean up this country by getting rid of the rats that touch our children.' I felt my blood freeze, my stomach contract, and I could only reply that I appreciated his offer but I didn't believe in violence. ... [I] understood that this hit man for the drug dealers was offering to assassinate Mario Marin, the governor of the State of Puebla, and his associate, Kamel Nacif, who had incarcerated and tortured me in 2005 to persuade me to retract the contents of my book, *The Demons of Eden*, an investigation of an international child pornography ring run by their accomplice Jean Succar Kuri (Cacho 2012: 144-145).

Obviously, this was an extraordinary situation to be in for any journalist: being called by a cartel assassin 'the bravest woman in this country' and given an offer to assassinate the very people who were not only responsible for her torture, rape and threats of death, but the kidnapping and rapes of countless innocent children. Not surprisingly, she made clear that she would not accept his offer.

Analysis Rather than Moral Condemnation

Beyond the compelling first-person narrative, what Cacho does extraordinarily well is to eschew simple moral condemnations in favour of analysis of real-life consequences of neoliberalism, the economic incentives that exist for people to engage in human trafficking and the international market of sex slavery.

In *Slavery, Inc.*, Cacho examines sex tourism and the concept of masculinity that demands sex-for-money without consequence; the pimp (the economic incentive to become one, but also the methods of conditioning kidnapped girls and 'breaking' them into becoming sex slaves); the protection rackets (from mafias but also corrupt

48

government officials and police); the traffickers themselves (the supply-side of the economy); the money-laundering (without which the market would not exist) and, of course, the women and girls themselves.

She writes simply: 'We cannot understand this criminal business unless we follow the money trail...' (2012: 7) and that in order to '... understand how human slavery works, we need to accept that the mafia runs businesses, that prostitution is an industry, and that women, girls and boys are commodities being sold' (ibid: 147). But, avoiding any Eurocentric evaluation of sex slavery, she argues:

> It is necessary to understand the socio-economic situation of the women and girls in each region, as well as the cultural perceptions of sexuality and violence. It is also important to take into account, in each case, how globalization and the assimilation of religious values have affected the sexual experiences of people of all ages (ibid: 227).

Allowing Women and Girls the Space to Speak

In addition, Cacho studiously avoids the temptation to narrate the stories of the survivors, instead allowing the exploited women and girls space to speak for themselves. There is, of course, a very long, important history of slave testimonials, especially in the abolitionist presses in the US during the trans-Atlantic slave trade, where it became clear that the power of individual accounts of slavery were much more potent if these were written in the first-person rather than narrated by (mostly white, male) abolitionists. Chief among these is that of Frederick Douglass (1818-1895) and, in fact, the first edition of his *Freedom's Journal* in 1827 includes the following quotation from John Brown Russwurm (1799-1851) on the masthead: 'We wish to plead our own cause. Too long have others spoken for us. Too long has the public been deceived by misrepresentations in things which concern us dearly' (Bales 2008: 2).

Cacho is certainly sensitive to this, writing: 'I will not attempt to narrate their stories based on the caregivers' moral evaluations or on the authorities' moral panic and doublespeak' (Cacho 2016: 65). In fact, some first-person passages from survivors are pages in length, demonstrating her dedication to providing ample space to recount fully not only the horrors of being a sex slave but the manner in which it happened, who they were before they were victimised, and how they have managed to rehabilitate afterwards. One example is Arely who recounts, in four pages of unedited testimonial, how she went from helping her grandmother sell *empanadas* (baked or fried pastry) on the streets of Maracaibo, Venezuela, to being 'tricked' when what she thought was a modelling job in Mexico turned out to be a debt-bondage scheme that forced her into prostitution. She ends her account by telling Cacho:

> … and I was punished. No food for two days. No chance of seeing anyone. Then I behaved. They were right: what did I have to return to in Venezuela? To fucking poverty on the street, without money for my studies … if a person has no opportunities, she does what others tell her to do (Cacho 2016: 124-125).

Challenging Some Feminist Assumptions – and Redefining Masculinity

Finally, Cacho engages with critical cultural theory, demanding feminists and sociologists account for some unexamined assumptions: for instance, how legalising prostitution might 'empower' women, or how pornography is a sign of 'liberated' sexuality. She counters that it may be the case that Western, liberal, feminist concepts about sex only serve to perpetuate the international sex slavery market. In an interview she makes the point that before she wrote *Slavery, Inc.*, she was 'open to the idea of legalising and regulating prostitution, and had listened to many academics and feminists who advocated it' (Saner 2012). But then her investigation into the global reach of the market changed her mind:

> … the more I travelled and the more women I interviewed, the more worried I got. I'm absolutely convinced that all forms of prostitution are just a way of normalising gender discrimination and violence against women, and women are 'trained' to become prostitutes because they are objects in a society that wants to have ghettoes of women who can be raped (ibid).

Here she posits a key question to feminists and sociologists: can Western, liberal feminism tolerate a system which demands 'ghettos of women who can be raped?' Because, according to her, this is exactly the end result of legalised prostitution. Of course, the counter-argument goes that some women enter into prostitution willingly, that legalising prostitution will take 'pimps' out of the equation and that the exchange of money for sex is not rape – it's a form of labour and should be re-defined as 'work'. However, Cacho is not fully convinced of this argument, maintaining that she does not really believe women can 'choose' to become a prostitute: 'In order to make a choice, you really need to have opportunities and options. If you don't, you are not really choosing, you are just getting by' (ibid). Neither is she convinced that legalising prostitution will eliminate 'pimps' and traffickers:

> The business is structured to control and exploit. On the one hand, it provides men throughout the world with what women and girls refuse to give them for free – sex without rules, obedience and subjugation. On the other hand, it enriches a few at the cost of many. It is naïve to believe that by legalising prostitution the mafias will stop engaging in the sexual exploitation of children, adolescents and adults on a transnational level (Cacho 2012: 237).

To Cacho, the root of the problem – and here is precisely where she goes further than most journalists, indeed most 'experts' in any field writing about the subject from privileged positions – lies in the failure of feminism to create a new, updated version of masculinity in the unceasing demands of neoliberal economics. Regarding the first cause, she writes that there is a 'backlash of women's liberation' where 'challenging the traditional paradigms of masculinity ... has angered millions of men. In almost all cultures there are sexist values that have remained unchanged. They have reinforced patriarchal relationships that require obedience and use violence to exercise control over women' (ibid: 198).

These angry men become the clients who seek out women in cultures and countries with '...weak judicial systems where there are "loving and submissive women"' (ibid: 228) who can be bought for sex. Of course, these women are not 'loving and submissive', they are bought and sold, trafficked, trained and conditioned to appear as such, but in the final analysis, they are *slaves*. Rather, what she claims is needed is to reconceptualise masculinity, minus the misogyny and normalisation of violence: 'A new masculine revolution is necessary. We need a new generation of men, not warriors, not armed, not threatening divine punishment, not violent, but men who possess a strong sense of progress and justice' (ibid: 222).

Confronting Neoliberalism

Regarding neoliberalism, or what she terms the 'dehumanising market economy', she writes: 'The capitalist rules of free trade have provided the mafia with countless opportunities to create new routes for the

trafficking of goods and services between countries and continents...'
and that the market for humans itself '...shows the weakness of global
capitalism and the disparity created by the most powerful countries'
economic rules.' This, in turn, 'reveals the normalization of human
cruelty and the culture that has encouraged it' where sex slaves '... are
bought, sold and re-sold like raw materials in any given industry, like
social waste, like trophies and gifts' (Cacho 2012: 2-3).

She continues: 'It is globalization's Achilles' heel: the inequality of
cultures, economics and legal systems, as well as the disparity in
intervention capabilities among countries and regions...' (ibid: 90). In
her work she demands that, if we really want to understand the
phenomenon, we must take into account the systemic imperatives –
economic, political, sociological – that drive the market; we must
forego moral denunciations as well as temptations to legalise, and thus
normalise, a market in human cruelty. And we must finally, and fully,
listen to the stories of the women and girls themselves:

> Beyond opinions and sociological hypothesis are the facts: these
> women and girls show us the route like sailors in the middle of
> the night who point to land and warn of the obstacles that must
> be faced in order to arrive there alive and on time (ibid: 90).

Conclusion: Moving Beyond Journalism into Activism

Regarding the global market in sex trafficking – the 'Lydia Cacho
cause'– she provides a model not only for journalists but also for those
wishing to move beyond journalism into activism. She founded and
directs the Comprehensive Women's Care Centre (Centro Integral de
Atención a las Mujeres), in Mexico and has always maintained a
careful separation between her journalism and the activities of the
shelter, refusing to take a salary as an activist:

> Ever since we opened the shelter I decided I would never have
> a salary as a human rights advocate. We were working towards
> getting public money invested in our organization, so I found it
> unethical to receive public money as an activist while
> continuing to investigate and write about gender issues,
> fighting the powers that be (Cacho 2016: 33).

All this she has done at great personal cost, as death threats continue,
the Mexican government '... does nothing' (McGeough 2014) and the
situation for women and girls around the world continues to worsen.

In an interview with Paul McGeough (himself no stranger to violence as war correspondent for the *Sydney Morning Herald*), he writes:

> Lydia Cacho is a journalist, an activist and advocate, a helper and a carer. Is she a victim? She brightens: 'No: I'm a survivor and that entails certain responsibilities. The circumstances of my life have offered me a glimpse of the ugliest side of a monster and have put me in a position to reveal its most savage dimensions' (ibid).

Yet she remains undeterred:

> I have investigated all manner of mafias throughout my career as a journalist, writer, and defender of human rights. The deaths of esteemed colleagues have marked the passing years, and their bravery is a daily inspiration to me. I have been kidnapped, jailed, and persecuted for many years ... I am one of thousands of activists and journalists who refuse to stand silently by in the face of such atrocities... (Cacho 2016: 2).

Lydia Cacho is, indeed, a model for anyone who wishes to become a journalist: she is a warrior for the cause and she will not be silenced.

References

Bales, Kevin and Trodd, Zoe (2008) *To Plead Our Own Cause: Personal Stories by Today's Slaves*, Ithaca, NY: Cornell University Press

Cacho, Lydia (2004) *Los Demonios Del Edén* [*The Demons of Eden*], Mexico City: Debolsillo

Cacho, Lydia (2012) *Slavery, Inc.: The Untold Story of International Sex Trafficking*, London: Portobello Books

Cacho, Lydia (2016) *Infamy: How One Woman Brought an International Sex Trafficking Ring to Justice*, Berkeley, CA: Soft Skull Press

International Labour Office (2017) *ILO Report: Global Estimates of Modern Slavery, Forced Labor and Forced Marriage*, Geneva: International Labour Office. Available online at https://www.ilo.org/wcmsp5/groups/public/---dgreports/---dcomm/documents/publication/wcms_575479.pdf

McGeough, Paul (2014) The defiant one, *Sydney Morning Herald*, 14 August. Available online at https://www.smh.com.au/world/the-defiant-one-20140818-3dv6y.html

Salas, Antonio (2004) *El Año Que Trafiqué Con Mujeres* [The Year I Trafficked Women], Madrid: Planeta

Saner, Emine (2012) Mexican journalist Lydia Cacho: 'I Don't Scare Easily', *Guardian*, 31 August. Available online at https://www.theguardian.com/world/2012/sep/01/lydia-cacho-mexican-journalist-interview

Saviano, Roberto (2012) Foreword: The power of ethics, Cacho, Lydia, *Slavery, Inc.*, London: Portobello Books

Vulliamy, Ed (2015) They want to erase journalists in Mexico, *Guardian*, 11 April. https://www.theguardian.com/world/2015/apr/11/mexico-fearless-journalist-lydia-cacho

Note on the Author

Todd Schack, PhD., is Associate Professor of Journalism and Media Studies, Ithaca College, New York. His work focuses on literary journalism, graphic nonfiction and the dark side of neoliberalism.

Chapter 6

Sex Crimes, Cover-Ups – and Conspiracy Theories

Child sexual abuse is now relatively common in the news but, as Claire Konkes writes, journalists must grapple with the complexity and ambiguity in these stories to avoid sensationalist coverage.

In 2009, the media reported that a Tasmanian independent politician, Terry Martin, was arrested for having sex with a 12-year-old girl. The girl was advertised as 'Angela 18, new in town' and sold by her mother and a man, Gary Devine, to between 100 and 200 men over four weeks. While the two who sold the child were jailed, all but one of the men who allegedly paid to have sex with her escaped arrest. This was because Tasmanian law at the time provided a defence of 'mistake as to age' allowing the accused to argue they had a mistaken but reasonable belief that the child was 18-years-old: after all, she was advertised in the local newspaper. Outrage erupted about why so many escaped convictions, including allegations of institutional cover-up and 'rumours that well-known figures such as lawyers, politicians and high-profile sportsmen might be among the suspects' (Neales 2010).

While the crimes against the girl are peculiar to the Australian island state of Tasmania, similar outrage was occurring elsewhere: Australia was on the cusp of its *Royal Commission into Institutional Responses to Child Sexual Abuse* (which led to the 2018 conviction of Cardinal George Pell for child sex offences); and the Irish government had just released reports (such as Murphy et al. 2009 and Ryan et al. 2009) into clerical child sexual abuse. In Britain, investigations into child sexual exploitation in Rochdale (see Berelowitz et al. 2013) and Rotherham (see Jay 2013) were revealing the extent to which social attitudes towards sexually active young people led police, social workers and others to ignore organised criminal activity. This refusal to see and act on allegations and rumour is described by Commissioner Sue Berelowitz as a culture of 'wilful blindness' (Ramesh 2014) and a 'conspiracy of silence' protecting the perpetrators and those who chose not to report them (Berelowitz et al. 2012). Amid these scandals, allegations in the UK against media entertainer Jimmy Savile in 2012 led to investigations into how both individuals and institutions contribute to the concealment of these abuses (see Gray and Watt 2013). All of these cases are examples of organised sexual abuse: that is the coordinated sexual abuse of children by multiple perpetrators (see Salter 2017). And some of them include the challenging problem of children involved in the exchange of sex for money or other favours.

These cases presented journalists with the challenge of representing how the social and institutional *mechanisms* enable perpetrators to commit such crimes and, in turn, allowed others to turn a blind-eye to the abuse. News stories often contain the tension between those seeking visibility and those seeking to control revelation (Lester and Hutchins 2012), but such stories can lead to claims of conspiracy, cover-up and witch hunts.

For journalists sifting through what is known and unknown, the frustratingly unverifiable becomes part of the job (see Tiffen 1999 33; Chomsky 2005). Yet, conspiracies do occur and considering alternative explanations to events that include wilful deception to serve a small group of people's interests is not irrational (Coady 2012). Conspiracy is a common term used in law and, further, reporting on cosy relationships, secret business deals and compromised officials are grist for the mill for journalists (Konkes and Lester 2017). In their review of the emerging prevalence of organised child sexual abuse, Middleton et al. (2014: 23-24) point to a 'parallel universe that is very close' that some 'will assign to the category of conspiracy'. Adding to the complexity of this picture are the crimes in which children appear to be complicit; where their abuse occurs in an apparent transaction for money or other favours, and where their status as children is made ambiguous because of their sexualisation.

The media, particularly news media, can serve to make this 'parallel universe' visible. As Thompson (2005: 49) observes, achieving 'visibility through the media is to gain a kind of presence or recognition in the public space' and, once in the public space, the mechanisms of secrecy are better understood and dismantled. This act of giving visibility to the unseen is the territory of many forms of journalism, including investigative journalism, but also other forms of reporting that examine and challenge social attitudes and assumptions. In the case of organised child sexual abuse, journalism is already recognised as not only instrumental in exposing these crimes, but for giving victims a voice and for applying the political pressure required for change. For instance, in Ireland, news coverage about clerical child sexual abuse is regarded as being 'generally well done' and 'absolutely necessary' (Auge et al. 2010: 67), and sustained media coverage highlighted Jimmy Savile's crimes as more victims came forward (Gray and Watt 2013). But reporting on child sexual abuse is also criticised for its sensationalism – and for provoking moral panics and witch-hunts (Salter 2017). These criticisms raise questions about how journalists are to challenge the various social and institutional mechanisms that protect perpetrators of child sexual exploitation without descending into sensationalism and other forms of misinformation.

Seeing the Crimes

While journalism serves to shift child sexual abuse from a shameful secret to a public issue (Kitzinger 2001: 100), reports with clear narratives of innocence and wickedness are more familiar than stories about children who appear to be complicit or 'willing' participants. Indeed, these crimes can be a 'minefield of ambiguity, inconsistency, and moralism around children and sex' (Grant et al. 2000:71; see also O'Connell Davidson 2005). Revelations during the 1970s about organised child sexual abuse tended to associate the crimes with paedophile or sex rings (Jenkins 2001) and were often discredited for being exaggerated (see Salter 2017). But in recent years, journalists in Britain and elsewhere have begun to highlight the deliberate organisation of these crimes.

Crimes involving children who exchange payment for sex, and the circumstances that enable this criminal activity, require a shift from the stereotype of the 'innocent 'or 'unknowing child' without drawing on language that represents the child as a 'willing sex worker' (McAlinden 2013) or 'an accomplice to his or her own sexual abuse' (Goddard et al. 2005: 281). Before the 1970s, the media often represented children as both seducers and victims (Zelizer 1985) with the sexual abuse of children regarded as a 'rather un-noteworthy form of sexual excess or deviation' (Angelides 2005: 272). The representation of the child as the seducer is epitomised in Nabokov's *Lolita* (1980 [1955]) in which Humbert Humbert defends his desire for his twelve-year-old step daughter Lolita by portraying her, rather than himself, as deviant. She is different to other children, he argues, because 'between the age limits of nine and fourteen there occur maidens who ... reveal their true nature which is not human, but nymphic' (ibid: 16). This idea of the desirability and complicity of the sexually willing child remains a stereotype that locates male desire for pubescent girls as normal, although transgressive. For instance, Christopher Hitchens (2005), in an essay on the enduring appeal of *Lolita*, suggested 'a common joking phrase among adult men, when they see nymphets on the street or in the park or, nowadays, on television and in bars, is "Don't even think about it"' (Hitchens 2005). This trope is deliberately blind to the inequity and power imbalance between the child that needs or wants something in exchange for sex and the adults who participate in the transaction. Significantly, the review into the abuse that occurred in Rochdale in the UK (Berelowitz et al. 2012: 47) found that children and young people were frequently described by welfare professionals as being 'promiscuous', 'liking the glamour', 'prostituting herself', being 'sexually available' and 'asking for it', and concluded that 'this labelling reflects a worrying perspective ... that children are complicit in, and hence responsible for, their own abuse'. Similarly, an independent inquiry into the case of the Tasmanian child sold to more than 100 men noted that 'police treatment of the absence/presence of consent in underage sex may have confused and distracted Child Protection Services from the risk' (Mason 2010: 7).

Seeing a Conspiracy of Silence

In reporting crime and other social problems, journalists routinely highlight the wrong-doing, ascribe blame and finally propose remedial action (Altheide 1997). In the case of Tasmania, for example, journalists represented the crime against the 12-year-old girl as being the result of child neglect and inadequate child protection systems (see Konkes and Lester 2016). Later coverage highlighted how social and institutional attitudes prevented justice being served and how those accused – identified by police using phone records – avoided prosecution. In this vacuum, speculation, criticism and allusions to a cover-up remained largely unchallenged and thus, allegations of a conspiracy and cover-up emerged.

Conspiracy theories can be locations for investigating how effectively the powerful attempt to influence public debate and, in turn, how effectively news media represent or challenge the communication strategies of the powerful (Jolley and Douglas 2014; Pelkmans and Machold 2011). Husting and Orr (2007:147) caution against the quick dismissal of conspiracy theories because 'mechanisms that define the limits of the sayable must continually be challenged' (see also Eldridge 1999).

Conclusion

For journalists reporting on organised child sexual abuse and exploitation the challenge is to find ways to describe the social and institutional mechanisms which the perpetrators exploit to ensure their abuse occurs 'unseen'. Journalists, then, have the choice to report on child abuse to promote more equitable and effective child protection policies and practices or to slip into simplistic or sensational coverage that falls back on old assumptions and stereotypes of childhood innocence.

References

Angelides, Steven (2005) The emergence of the paedophile in the late twentieth century, *Australian Historical Studies*, Vol. 36, No.126 pp 272-295

Altheide, David (1997) The news media, the problem frame and the production of fear, *Sociological Quarterly*, Vol. 38, No. 4 pp 647-668

Auge, Andrew, Fuller, Louise, Littleton, John and Maher, Eamon (2010) After the Ryan and Murphy Reports: A roundtable on the Irish Catholic Church, *New Hibernia Review*, Vol. 14, No. 1 pp 59-77

Berelowitz, Sue, Firmin, Carlene, Edwards, Gareth and Gulyurtlu, Sandra (2012) *'I Thought I Was the Only One. The Only One in the World': The Office of the Children's Commissioner's Inquiry into Child Sexual Exploitation in Gangs and Groups – Interim Report*, London: Office of the Children's Commissioner, England

Coady, David (2012) *What to Believe Now: Applying Epistemology to Contemporary Issues*, Malden: Blackwell

Chomsky, Noam (2005) Simple truths, hard problems: Some thoughts on terror, justice, and self-defence, *Philosophy*, Vol. 80. No. 1 pp 5-28

Eldridge, John (1999) *Risk, Society and the Media: Now You See It, Now You Don't*, London: Longman

Gray, David, and Watt, Peter (2013) *'Giving Victims a Voice': A joint MPS and NSPCC Report into Allegations of Sexual Abuse Made Against Jimmy Savile under Operation Yewtree*, London: Metropolitan Police Service

Hitchens, Christopher (2005) Hurricane Lolita, *Atlantic Monthly*, December. Available online at http://www.theatlantic.com/magazine/archive/2005/12/hurricane-lolita/304386/

Husting, Gina and Orr, Martin (2007) Dangerous machinery: 'Conspiracy theorist' as a transpersonal strategy of exclusion, *Symbolic Interaction, Vol.* 30, No. 1 pp 127-150

Jay, Alexis (2013) *Independent Inquiry into Child Sexual Exploitation in Rotherham 1997-2013*, Rotherham: Rotherham Metropolitan Borough Council

Jenkins, Phillip (2001) How Europe discovered its sex-offender crisis, Best, Joel (ed.) *How Claims Spread: Cross-National Diffusion of Social Problems*, NY: Aldine de Gruyter pp 147-168

Jolley, Daniel and Douglas, Karen M. (2014) The social consequences of conspiracism: Exposure to conspiracy theories decreases intentions to engage in politics and to reduce one's carbon footprint, *British Journal of Psychology, Vol.* 105, No. 1 pp 35-56

Konkes, Claire and Lester, Libby (2016) Justice, politics and the social usefulness of news, *Crime, Media, Culture*, Vol. 12, No. 1 pp 17-35

Konkes, Claire and Lester, Libby (2017) Incomplete knowledge, rumour and truth seeking: When conspiracy theories become news, *Journalism Studies*, Vol. 18, No. 7 pp 826-844

Lester, Libby and Hutchins, Brett (2012) The power of the unseen: Environmental conflict, the media and invisibility, *Media, Culture & Society*, Vol. 34 No. 7 pp 847-863

Mason, Paul (2010) *'She Will Do Anything to Make Sure She Keeps the Girls': Inquiry into the Circumstances of a 12-year-old Child under Guardianship of the Secretary*, Hobart: Commissioner for Children

McAlinden, Anne-Marie (2013) An inconvenient truth: Barriers to truth recovery in the aftermath of institutional child abuse in Ireland, *Legal Studies*, Vol. 33, No.2 pp 189-214

Middleton, Warwick, Stavropoulos, Pam, Dorahy, Martin J., Krüger, Christa, Lewis-Fernández, Roberto, Martínez-Taboas, Alfonso, Sar, Vedat and Brand, Bethany (2014) Institutional abuse and societal silence: An emerging global problem, *Australian & New Zealand Journal of Psychiatry*, Vol. 48. No. 1 pp 22-25

Murphy, Yvonne, Mangan, Ita and O'Neill, Hugh (2009) *Report of the Commission of Investigation: Report into the Catholic Archdiocese of Cloyne, Department of Justice and Equality*, Ireland

Nabokov, Vladimir (1980 [1955]) *Lolita*, London: Penguin

Neales, Sue (2010) Innocence stripped naked of all dignity, *Mercury*, 4 October p. 12

O'Connell Davidson, Julia (2005) *Children in the Global Sex Trade*, Cambridge: Polity Press

Pelkmans, Mathijs and Machold, Rhys (2011) Conspiracy theories and their truth trajectories, *Focaal*, Vol. 59 pp 66-80

Ramesh, R. (2014) Culture of denial leaving UK children at risk of serious abuse, *Guardian*, 28 August. Available online at https://www.theguardian.com/uk-news/2014/aug/27/culture-denial-rotherham-sexual-abuse-berelowitz-police

Salter, Michael (2017) Organised sexual abuse in the media, Pontel, Henry (ed.) *Oxford Research Encyclopaedia of Criminology and Criminal Justice*, Oxford University Press: Oxford

Thompson, John. B. (2005) The new visibility, *Theory, Culture & Society*, Vol. 22, No. 6 pp 31-51

Tiffen, Rodney (1999) *Scandals: Media, Politics and Corruption in Contemporary Australia*, Sydney: UNSW Press

Zelizer, Barbie (1985) *Pricing the Priceless Child*, New York: Basic Books

Note on the Author

Dr Claire Konkes lectures at the University of Tasmania's Media School where her teaching and research interests focus on the influence of news media in public debate about social change and law reform.

Chapter 7

The Orgy Next Door: An Exploration of Ethics and Methods in Gay Talese's *The Voyeur's Motel*

In 2016, Gay Talese, the eminent American literary journalist, published a book based on the journals of a self-confessed voyeur – involving copulation, drug dealing, incest and even murder. Not surprisingly, a massive controversy erupted. Julie Wheelwright examines the issues.

In the summer of 2016, Gay Talese, the journalist Tom Wolfe credited with founding the New Journalism, appeared at the centre of a controversy (Talese 1997: 171). The author of fourteen books, including such classics as *The Kingdom and the Power* (1969), *Honor Thy Father* (1971), *Thy Neighbor's Wife* (1980) and his 1966 *Esquire* profile, 'Frank Sinatra has a cold', Talese's reputation had a long way to fall. Novelist Mario Puzo declared him 'the best nonfiction writer in America' (Talese 2011a: back cover) while Barbara Lounsberry called him 'a reporter's reporter who is revered by fellow writers' (Lounsberry 2003: vii).

More recently, doubt was cast on these accolades, however, with the publication of his investigative work, *The Voyeur's Motel*. Based on the journals of the title's self-confessed voyeur (Talese 2016c), the book made factual claims to Gerald Foos's observations of copulating couples at the Aurora, Colorado, a motel that he purported to own from 1965 to 1995. Foos also recorded witnessing criminal behaviour: domestic abuse, drug dealing, incest and even a murder. The *New Yorker* ran a lengthy extract in April 2016 (Talese 2016d: 40-55), attracting widespread media attention, with producer-director Steven Spielberg purchasing the film rights, and a planned national book tour.

However, Paul Farhi's *Washington Post* investigation revealed major discrepancies between events described in *The Voyeur's Motel* and information found in public records. Foos had, in fact, sold the

Colorado motel in 1980 and only reacquired it eight years later. Farhi also discovered that the murder Foos recorded in his journal bore a striking resemblance to the case of Irene Cruz who was murdered in November 1977, not in Foos's motel but in a Denver hotel (Farhi 2016a). Foos was exposed as an unreliable narrator despite Talese's experience of joining him on the motel's viewing platform, in January 1980, to verify his claims. When confronted, Talese says: 'I should not have believed a word he said,' adding that he would not promote the book because its 'credibility was down the toilet' (Farhi 2016b). However, a publisher's retraction quickly followed, quoting Talese saying: 'I am not disavowing the book, and neither is my publisher. ... If, down the line, there are details to correct in later editions, we'll do that' (Farhi 2016c).

Aside from the book's factual inaccuracies, criticism focused on concerns about the ethics of including Foos's observations of the unconsenting couples (Lehr 2016c). Reviewers raised similar questions in 1981 about the narrative reliability and lack of ethical boundaries in Talese's research and writing of *Thy Neighbor's Wife* (Talese 1981e), a social history of America's sexual revolution. In an epilogue to this 512-page volume, Talese admits both to having sexual relationships with female subjects interviewed during his investigation and to managing a Manhattan massage parlour. Fellow journalists, authors and feminists were excoriating in their comments. Talese says of the experience: 'I was made to feel like I was an essentially wicked, perverted person. ... It was my version of a scarlet letter' (Roiphe 2009: 85-86).

However, despite this critical lambasting, Talese returns to the subject of sexual practice in *The Voyeur's Motel*. Here, he includes the journals in which Foos recorded his own voyeuristic experiences, some of which Talese originally considered including in *Thy Neighbor's Wife*. While Talese questions his reactions to the material throughout the 2016 book, he proceeded to publish descriptions of the couples, without their knowledge, and whose consent could have been sought because Foos possessed their real names and addresses. Another concern was whether Talese was complicit in Foos's crimes, not only by failing to report them but by providing the voyeur with a media platform and thereby escalating his compulsive behaviour (Walsh-Childers 2016). While *Thy Neighbor's Wife* is a much longer, more considered – albeit problematic – book, *The Voyeur's Motel*, while a complement in subject, fails the public interest test. Moreover, both may have caused harm to the investigated subjects.

There are lessons here for literary journalists and scholars of literary journalism interested in the practices and ethics of immersion. Broadly, the issues relate to the journalist's need to consider the impact that their status and behaviour may have on their subjects. If the journalist is not transparent about how his or her very presence frames the relationship to the group or individuals studied, the result may produce an unreliable text. If the motives are falsified, the testimony may become manipulative and the resulting narrative may fail – as I argue in the case of *The Voyeur's Motel* – that of public interest.

The Ethics of Immersive Journalism

Walt Harrington describes journalists as the 'junkyard dogs of ethnography' and while the suspicion may be mutual, these respective practices share many characteristics (Harrington 2003: 90). Journalists who employ immersive techniques involve themselves in the lives and events of their subjects: the writer may live with his or her subjects, let the action unfold naturally, collect material through the observation of sensory details, record overheard dialogue and watch for small events and details that evoke their stories' themes (ibid: 92-94). However, despite the intimacy of the experience, according to Anne Hull, journalists must 'minimize your presence', remembering that 'you are not one of them', 'you are ever the infidel' who must preserve the need to 'check people out' (Hull 2007: 41-42). Robin Hemley and others, while acknowledging the individual aspect of this practice, argue that the immersive writer must use the public interest test when making methodological and ethical decisions (Hemley 2012: 150). There is a shared understanding that the journalist's primary responsibility is to the reader and to the author's employer rather than to the investigated subject.

Throughout an immersive journalistic investigation, a writer will attempt to preserve a formal distance (Hull's notion of remaining 'ever the infidel') in order to construct the narrative. In this scenario, the writer must become separate from the subject in order to view the experience for the consumption of the imagined reader. Anne Hermann challenges this assumption of distance, however, arguing that the journalist in the field 'cannot remain a detached observer and narrator, but must become an immersed partaker' (Hermann 2016: 269). The hybrid of 'ethnographic reporters' inevitably transcends 'not only professional conventions and reporting habits but also their own demographic profiles' by 'exchanging the traditional skeptical attitude with an empathetic one' (Cramer and McDevitt 2004: 131; Hermann 2016: 269). Journalists must balance respect for their subjects' vulnerabilities while retaining authorial control: the journalists' version of what they witnessed, how they have understood it and what it means.

Talese reflects on his process of immersion in his essay, 'Origins of a nonfiction writer' (Talese 1997: 166-196). A pivotal influence in his development as a journalist were hours spent as a child observing his mother with her female customers at her dress boutique in Ocean City, New Jersey. The shop was 'a kind of talk show', he writes, where his mother's 'engaging manner and well-timed questions' drew out intimate confessions from her clients. Talese 'used to pause and eavesdrop ... to listen with patience and care, and never to interrupt', techniques which he later parlayed into interviews (Talese 2011a: 167-168). Immersion, for Talese, demands a considerable amount of time and the writer's physical presence. Once consent is obtained and subjects agree to have their real names used, Talese is free to describe a group or individual's behaviour through his own idiosyncratic perspective rather than as a representative of the subject or group.

The Voyeur's Motel reveals the flaws in this argument since Talese selectively defined whose consent would be obtained (Foos's, not the motel guests') and, despite an increased openness about his methods and a more reflective narrative mode, failed to read the psychological warning signs. Moreover, Talese's identification with Foos suggests a reticence to explore his own writer's subjectivity which may have led him to this suspension of critical judgement.

The Voyeur's Motel (2016)

Thy Neighbor's Wife and *The Voyeur's Motel* share a history. Foos was originally in correspondence with Talese as a potential subject in 1980 and had, over the years, continued to send the writer his journals. So it might be regarded as a companion volume that deals with the same intimate subject matter while raising a fresh set of ethical concerns. Among them is the writer's own preoccupation with voyeurism: in *The Voyeur's Motel*, he compares his journalistic motives and methods to those of the voyeur, drawing a distinction between 'the people I observed' and those he 'reported on [and] had given me their consent' (Talese 2016c: 5). He makes a parallel comment, perhaps unconsciously, in 'Origins of a nonfiction writer' where he describes himself as overhearing 'many people discussing candidly with my mother what they had earlier avoided' in the dress shop, another form of watching that is central to his evolving identity as a journalist (Talese 2011a: 168). The unseen narrator depends entirely on context and, in the service of journalism, is entirely justified.

Talese describes how he is driven by curiosity, after receiving Foos's letter, to meet at his Denver motel on 23 January 1980 (Talese 2016c: 8). After their first meeting, Talese writes up his daily impressions about his encounters, a long-established practice (ibid: 18). He provides a detailed physical description of Foos, his mannerisms and his character, even though Talese considers: 'What could I see in his attic that I had not already seen as the researching writer of *Thy Neighbor's Wife* and a frequenter of Sandstone's swinging couples' ballroom [where orgies took place]?' (ibid). He presses on despite such doubts.

There are several moments of such reflection throughout the book where Talese contemplates the ethics of publishing Foos's platform observations, justified as Foos 'indulging his curiosity within the boundaries of his own property, and since his guests were unaware of his voyeurism, they were not affected by it ... there's no violation of privacy if no one complains' (ibid: 26). Once the behaviour is rationalised, Talese joins Foos on the platform (and returns 'a number of additional times'), to watch couples copulating (ibid: 37). While Talese admits this activity is 'very illegal' and reflects on his complicity 'in this strange and distasteful project', he decides that, because Foos must remain anonymous, the material is unusable and returns to New York to begin his promotional tour for *Thy Neighbor's Wife* (ibid: 37).

Between 1980 and 1995, when the motel was sold, Foos, who compared himself to the sexologists Alfred Kinsey, William Masters and Virginia Johnson, became increasingly bored and frustrated, driving him to increasingly risky behaviour. For example, he planted sexual paraphernalia and pornography in a motel room and recorded whether his 'subjects' used them (ibid: 92) and followed female 'subjects' back to their homes, even making inquiries about one from a neighbour (ibid: 79, 83). Reading this material, in New York at a geographical and psychological distance, Talese wonders if 'voyeurs sometimes need escape from prolonged solitude by exposing themselves to other people (as Foos had done first with his wife, and later me), and then seek a larger audience as an anonymous scrivener of what they've witnessed?' (ibid: 36) This statement seems to suggest that Talese was aware that he may have been complicit in Foos's criminal behaviour as a celebrated writer publishing his accounts – which would then satisfy the voyeur's stated desire for 'a larger audience'.

Does it Pass the Test of Public Interest?

Critics of *The Voyeur's Motel* argue that Talese indeed violated journalistic ethics. Dick Lehr, writing in the *Huffington Post*, suggests that while his refusal to notify the authorities about violations of privacy, Talese's book fails the test of public interest. 'Promises reporters make to sources are a very big deal,' Lehr writes. 'It's a matter of trust, a promise so sacrosanct that many reporters would only consider breaking it in the rarest of exceptions' (Lehr 2016). But, for Lehr, Talese's concerns for the couples' privacy should have taken precedence over the writer's loyalty to his informant and he asks why Talese chose to believe Foos (ibid).

Is Criminal Behaviour Encouraged?

The second ethical issue arises over whether Talese, as the voyeur's constant reader and one who holds out the promise of an international readership for his 'research', encouraged his criminal behaviour. Kim Walsh-Childers argues that by respecting their confidentiality agreement, Talese allows Foos to subject hundreds, even thousands more guests to his voyeurism, judgement and scorn. Their years of correspondence affirmed Foos's behaviour, 'helping him maintain the myth that his actions served some higher purpose, some noble societal goal, rather than simply satisfying his own sexual desire' (Walsh-Childers 2016: 18). More disturbing is the possibility that Talese, as Foos's audience, influenced him to experiment with his guests in which violations of their privacy escalate – the sexual paraphernalia planted in their rooms, the stalking of female guests. Voyeurism, according to psychologists, is rarely a discrete clinical entity: many studies have found that perpetrators of voyeurism also engage in other forms of sexual deviance, including rape, paedophilia, exhibitionism and sadism (Adams 2016: 216-218).

Is the Journalist Too Identified with his Subject?

Not all of the commentators, however, agreed on the book's implications for journalistic practice. David L. Ulin, writing in the *Los Angeles Times*, argues that Talese probably relied too heavily on Foos as a narrator simply because of the author's 'desire to believe' this 'too good not to tell' story (Ulin 2016).

Lad Tobin, writing more broadly about Talese's methods in his *Esquire* article, 'Frank Sinatra has a cold', also concludes that, however unconscious, the author's fascination and identification with his subject is a primary framing device (Tobin 2010: 143-144).

Conclusions: On the Need for Psychological Insight

I would argue that Talese's references to his own voyeurism – as a boy in his mother's shop, as a journalist participating in the Sandstone orgies, with Foos in the motel – seep 'into almost everything he sees and says' in the book (Tobin 2010: 144). Ulin's view that Talese is motivated by a desire to relay Foos's 'too good not to tell' story ignores what Tobin uncovers: that the author's unconscious, over-identification with his subject causes him to suspend his critical judgement. Moreover, Talese's unresolved and conflicted feelings about his own sexual desires are played out in *Thy Neighbor's Wife*, another case where his ability to maintain distance – and judgement – collapses.

Talese's self-reflective mode in *The Voyeur's Motel* fails to address fully concerns about consent and transparency. The ethical questions are in sharp relief as Talese's behaviour condones his subject's crimes and even encourages the voyeur's sexually deviant behaviour to escalate. Perhaps the most vital message in this exploration into reporting on fraught territory of sexual intimacy is the need for psychological insight and an ability to face up to the raw honesty of our motivating psyches. As Phillip Lopate writes about the essential requirement for good personal writing, 'remorse is often the starting point ... whose working out brings the necessary self-forgiveness (not to mention self-amusement) that is necessary to help us outgrow shame' (Lopate 2013: 25). Whatever Talese's motivations that lay behind the years he has devoted to writing about sex, perhaps this self-understanding might have been a better and more ethical starting place.

References

Adams, Henry E. (2000) Voyeurism, Kazdin, Alan E. (ed.) *Encyclopedia of Psychology*, Washington, DC: American Psychological Association. New York, NY: Oxford University Press Vol. 8 pp 216-218

Cramer, Janet M. and McDevitt, Michael (2004) Ethnographic journalism, Hartin Iorio, Sharon (ed.) *Qualitative Research in Journalism: Taking it to the Streets*, Mahwah, NJ: Lawrence Erlbaum Associates pp 127-43

Farhi, Paul (2016a) The murder the *New Yorker* never mentioned, *Washington Post*, 13 April. Available online at https://www.washingtonpost.com/lifestyle/style/the-murder-the-new-yorker-never-mentioned, accessed on 14 June 2019

Farhi, Paul (2016b) Gay Talese renounces his lurid new book about a motel voyeur: 'Its credibility is down the toilet', *National Post*, 1 July 2016. Available online at http://news.nationalpost.com/arts/gay-talese-the-voyeurs-motel, accessed on 14 June 2019

Farhi, Paul (2016c) Motel voyeur tales face 'credibility' questions, *National Post*, 2 July 2016. Available online at http://0-library.pressdisplay.com.wam.city.ac.uk, accessed on 14 June 2019

Harrington, Walt (2003) What journalism can offer ethnography, *Qualitative Inquiry*, Vol. 9, No. 1 pp 90-104

Hemley, Robin (2012) *A Field Guide for Immersion Writing: Memoir, Journalism, and Travel*, Athens: University of Georgia Press

Hermann, Anne Kristine (2016) Ethnographic journalism, *Journalism: Theory, Practice and Criticism*, Vol. 17, No. 2 pp 260-278

Hull, Anne (2007) Being there, Kramer, Mark and Call, Wendy (eds) *Telling True Stories: A Nonfiction Writers' Guide from the Nieman Foundation at Harvard University*, New York: Plume pp 39-45

Lopate, Phillip (2013) *To Show and to Tell: The Craft of Literary Nonfiction*, London: Free Press

Lounsberry, Barbara (ed.) (2003) *The Gay Talese Reader: Portraits and Encounters*, New York: Walker

Roiphe, Katie (2009) Gay Talese, the art of nonfiction, No. 2, *Paris Review*, Vol. 189 pp 57-93. Available online at http://www.theparisreview.org/interviews/5925/the-art-of-nonfiction-no-2-gay-talese, accessed on 14 June 2019

Talese, Gay (2011a) Origins of a nonfiction writer, *Frank Sinatra Has a Cold and Other Essays*. London: Penguin pp 166-196

Talese, Gay (1978b) *The Kingdom and the Power: History of* The New York Times, New York: Doubleday

Talese, Gay (2016c) *The Voyeur's Motel*, London: Grove Press

Talese, Gay (2011d) The Voyeur's Motel, *New Yorker*, 11 April 2016 pp 40-55

Talese, Gay (1981e) *Thy Neighbor's Wife*, London: Pan

Tobin, Lad (2010) Gay Talese has a secret, *Fourth Genre: Explorations in Nonfiction*, Vol. 12, No. 2 pp 135-146

Ulin, David L. (2016) All manner of goings-on, *Los Angeles Times*, 10 July 2016

Walsh-Childers, Kim (2016) An ethical bind, *Huffington Post*, 14 April. Available online at http://www.huffingtonpost.com/the-conversation-us-the-murky-ethics-of-gay-t_b_9694344.html, accessed on 14 June 2019

Wolfe, Tom (1975) *The New Journalism: With an Anthology*, Wolfe, Tom and Johnson, E. W. (eds) London: Picador

Note on the Author

Julie Wheelwright, a broadcaster and journalist, is the author of several books of narrative nonfiction and has been programme director of the MA creative writing nonfiction at City, University of London, since 2007.

Chapter 8

Whores, Activists and Journalists

In Mexico, infuriated by the social and media stigmatisation, a collective of sex workers turned to journalism to tell their own stories,
Antonio Castillo writes.

Stigma and News Representation

Flor is a transgender sex worker. Her home is Mexico City, the gritty and anarchic urban enclave where 21 million live. It is also the capital of Mexico. She was 19 when she found a way to make a living. 'On a street I saw some men dressed as women who were standing there,' she says. She asked them what they were doing. 'Working,' they told her. 'At that moment I thought: I am from here.'

Flor is now 63. Her tale is one of the 16 personal stories published in *Putas, Activistas y Periodistas* (*Whores, Activists and Journalists*), a book, launched in 2018, whose gestation goes back to mid-2009 when Flor and other sex workers began learning the art and craft of journalism.

The book – and the incursion into journalism – was powered by the anger sex workers feel about their demonisation by Mexican media and society. The media – Flor says in the book – 'speak badly about us' and treat 'us as if we were the antichrist'. Day in and day out the Mexican press and electronic media portray sex workers as criminals, carriers of sexual diseases and an imminent danger to society.

In Mexico, the demonisation of sex workers is nothing new. However, it began to grow exponentially in the 1980s when the AIDS epidemic became a daily news story. This media representation is not unique to Mexico. Academic studies, such as the one conducted by Fong et al. (2013), show the mainstream media tends to construct sex workers and sex work as deviant and a threat to society. The 'press has used salacious photos of sex workers while disregarding their words and stories, and journalists repeatedly ask stigmatizing questions in order to push an agenda,' according to Lily O'Delia, a sex worker and writer (2016).

It doesn't take hours of research to realise that most of the stories involving sex workers are found in the crime and police section of the press. Writing about the reporting of sex workers in the Spanish press, Simón and Saiz point out (2018): 'In general terms, what we know about prostitution via the media is almost restricted to information about raids of alleged trafficking networks for the purpose of sexual exploitation.' The coverage, they write, is 'presented as successes in the fight against trafficking and prostitution, mixing both terms'.

It is likely that Flor has never read those academic findings. But on the streets of Mexico City she experiences them in the flesh. In *Whores, Activists and Journalists*, Flor remembers a painful event involving police brutality and appalling media coverage. It goes back to the 1970s when sex workers became – as she says – 'narco-demonised'. She was detained and the police took her to the police car.

'They took away my belongings and the little money I carried, they planted drugs on me and put a machine gun in my hand,' she remembers. 'With two or three bundles of drugs and a submachine gun in my hand, they took photos of me. The newspapers *La Prensa* and *El Sol de México* descended into yellow journalism writing about a "gang dedicated to prostitution".' In both newspapers she is portrayed as a thief and drug dealer.

Sex Work

In Mexico – in the context of unemployment, the absence of social security and miserable wages – prostitution is an important form of subsistence for many women. 'The growth of prostitution is linked to macroeconomic policies where rapid urbanization was encouraged at the expense of rural development,' says Jaime Alberto Moreno, spokesperson for the civil rights body, Street Brigade (Domínguez 2016).

It is estimated that in Mexico there are more than 800,000 people carrying out some form of sex work, either forced or voluntary (Montejo 2013). And in Mexico City it is estimated that 70,000 are engaged in prostitution – at least 18,000 of them are minors, between 15- and 17-years-old (Castillo 2016). The human rights body, Street Brigade, estimates that 70 per cent of the sex workers are women, 25 per cent transvestites, transsexuals and transgender while 5 per cent are men.

In June 2019, Mexico City lawmakers gave the green light to the decriminalisation of sex work in the capital, hoping it would be a first step in a crackdown on sex trafficking that traps thousands of Mexican women and children. The decriminalisation move divides opinions – some considering sex work a form of oppression of women and sexual minorities, while others see regulation as the only way to end abuses.

'Prostitution in Mexico is legal under federal law – with each of the 31 states enacting its own prostitution laws and policies,' writes Maya Oppenheim (2019). 'Although sex work is allowed in much of the country, states have different and at times unclear rules, which leads to workers frequently operating in legal vacuums that expose them to exploitation and trafficking by criminal gangs.'

In this context 'sex workers in Mexico are trapped in a legal limbo: individual prostitution by adults is not prohibited but also not regulated, and consequently some forms of work organisation (in apartments or clubs) can be considered to be "sexual exploitation" or "pandering"' (Lamas 2016).

Three 'normative' models of prostitution management frame the news coverage, public debate and public policy in Mexico. One model demands prohibition on the basis that prostitution is a crime; the second recommends its regulation because prostitution cannot be eradicated and hence has to be controlled; while the final model aims at its abolition, given the sexual discrimination suffered by women as victims of male exploitation (López and Mestre 2006: 67-68).

It is around these three 'normative management' models of prostitution that Mexican sex workers articulate their activism through their own brand of journalism. The Mexican Alliance of Sex Workers (AMETS) called for the voice of this sector of the population to be heard as laws are developed about prostitution. 'It's necessary to give us space and a voice because it's about our work, our daily subsistence. This work is the option that we choose among all those that exist to us. All of us here work because we want to and we want to keep it that way,' according to a statement by AMETS.

Not only in Mexico but around the world there is a growing sense that, as Beatriz Gimeno, a Spanish politician and LGBT rights activist, puts it: 'It is crucial to give voice to the prostitutes themselves, stop victimizing them, recognize their agency and respect the way they choose to escape poverty or to improve their living conditions; respect their choices' (2013).

It was only until recently that sex worker activists – such as Flor and her colleagues – used to cover their faces with masks when they wanted to be heard. Today 'without a sense of shame' sex workers are photographed and interviewed. This new visibility is one of the bi-products of an increasing political awareness that, combined with activism and journalism, make them writers of their own stories.

Whores and Journalists

The idea of a journalism workshop for sex workers began germinating in mid-2009. It was conceived inside a bus packed with sex workers. They were heading to Tlaxcala, a state in central Mexico, to participate in a National Meeting of Sex Workers. Among them were Gloria Muñoz Ramirez and Elvira Madrid.

Gloria Muñoz Ramirez is a well-known columnist of *La Jornada*, one of the most respected Mexican newspapers and one of the creators of Desinformémonos (Let's disinform), an independent media project. For Gloria Muñoz Ramirez, journalist and workshop facilitator, 'journalism can be exercised from below, by any person or group that decides to produce and disseminate information with a social objective and, above all, with an intention. Ours is clear: change the world, starting with our world' (Muñoz Ramirez and Avendaño 2018: 12).

Elvira Madrid is a sociologist and one of the founders of Brigada Callejera (Street Brigade) a non-profit civil organisation composed of sex workers, transgender and survivors of human trafficking. Created in 1995, Street Brigade installed journalism into the core of its work. It has established NotiCalle (News Streets) – a news agency staffed by sex workers who write about their stories, demands and grievances.

The book *Whores, Activists and Journalists* – published in 2018 – is the end result of a strategic collaboration between Desinformémonos and Brigada Callejera, and of almost seven years of a journalism training undertaken by a committed group of sex workers. The journalism workshops began with ten sex workers including women and transsexuals along with three members of the Street Brigade.

In her introduction to the book, Muñoz Ramirez remembers that the first workshops were held in a house owned by Street Brigade in Mapimí Street, in the Valle Gómez neighbourhood – just north of the city's historic centre. A few chairs and a small blackboard in the courtyard formed the humble journalism classroom. Years later the workshop moved to the offices of Desinformémonos in La Merced, a neighbourhood considered one of the main areas of sex work Mexico City.

It is in La Merced where Patricia Mérida Ortiz, 'Mérida', mainly worked as a sex worker. When she joined the journalism workshop she had more than 30 years' experience in the trade. She started at the age of 16. Now in her 50s, she is a wife, activist, mother, grandmother and journalist. 'I wanted to be a journalist to disseminate our realities and to make the world better,' she writes. 'To enter the minds of those who read my notes so they can really know what happens behind the street corners and why we are there' (Muñoz Ramirez and Avendaño 2018: 174).

Gloria Muñoz Ramirez, a journalist who has experienced threats to her life due to her work with indigenous communities and social movements, started the workshops on Mondays at 10am. 'No one arrived on time,' writes Muñoz Ramirez, who as a seasoned journalist was the ideal person to conduct the workshops. 'I was exasperated so we decided then to hold the meetings at 12 noon and the same thing happened,' she says. After realising the morning meetings were not feasible the workshop was moved to 3pm in the afternoon. 'Things got better from then on' (ibid: 10).

As in any journalism workshop, in the introductory sessions Muñoz Ramirez encouraged the participants to discuss – let's call it basic journalistic theoretical notions. What is journalism? she asked them. Then came the follow-up question: why do you want to do journalism? To this question there was one definite answer – as sex workers and activists they wanted to learn the art and craft of journalism to tell about their 'struggles and their dreams' (ibid: 12).

And as any respected journalism academic knows – theory is followed by practical activities. They first learned the art of note-taking and interviewing. It was hard work since the degree of education of the 'students' was as diverse as the number of participants – a few had only basic education while others had finished high school. 'No-one had ever used a computer, recorded for an interview or transcribed anything. You had to start from scratch,' Muñoz Ramirez remembers (ibid: 14).

In journalism schools we call it 'peer review' and this is what they did. They observed and corrected each other and, in the end, asked their interviewee to evaluate the work as reporters. The interviewee evaluation was 'the one that always mattered to us', says Muñoz

Ramirez. 'How did you feel during the interview? How did you feel about the questions? What do you think about our work as journalists? What do you think we lack? What would you modify?' These were the kinds of questions posed at the end of each session (ibid: 15).

Computer classes were held. They were needed to transcribe the testimonies of the participants: the sex workers were keen to tell their life stories. 'After having the testimonies and their transcripts, the editing stage came,' says Muñoz Ramirez. 'The strategy consisted of reading aloud each transcript, while correcting spelling and punctuation; leads were chosen, followed by narrative harmony; rhythm, sequences and coherence were sought in each interview.' They agreed to tell the stories using the 'vertical pronoun' – the first person (ibid: 16).

It was a journalistic 'learning process that took seven years', says Sandra Montiel Díaz. Now in her 40s, she began working as a sex worker at the age of 17. 'I never imagined that I would become a journalist,' she says. 'I want people to read notes about us that have truth, not like those that we often see in the news or on television.'

Montiel Díaz 'talonea' (or works the heels: Mexican jargon for street prostitution) in the corners of Tlalpan, is an avenue of Mexico City, which connects its historic centre with the southern zone. There, about 1,500 prostitutes work, a third of them transgender. Years ago while on the street a man threw acid on to her face. As a sex worker she feels proud. 'It's a work like any other,' she writes. 'A reporter uses his camera or recorder while I use my genitals' (ibid: 179).

During the journalism workshops, Montiel Díaz interviewed sex workers from Nicaragua and Honduras. They crossed the borders to Mexico to work. 'They told us their reality, how they are extorted, that sometimes not only are they are exploited by the owners of the bars, as they say in the news, but also by the authorities. I learnt that on the southern border of Mexico they are forced to pay for the compulsory monthly health checks that are supposed to be free.' She adds: 'They live constantly with the fear of deportation' (ibid: 182).

The journalism workshop changed the life of Montiel Díaz. It also changed her perspective on life. 'Now, as a journalist, I have a different approach to situations – I can go on a march to demand rights for us, and if there is violence from the authorities, I know how to take a picture, write a story, film a video,' she says. 'That way people can see how things are' (ibid: 184).

Journalism and truth are the main concerns of María Soledad Sánchez Toledo – one of the interviewers and one of the four co-authors of *Whores, Journalists and Activists*. A journalist who covers sex work, she says, 'must tell the truth'. 'If somebody likes sex work that is all good, but if somebody is forced into the work – it has to be said.' Indeed, all the 'trafficking, extortion, violence, disappearances, kidnapping, the murders and the mafia networks' have to be confronted. As a journalist, she wants to 'dignify the work of the comrades and help to rescue those who are there against their will' (ibid: 190).

The Book

The book *Whores, Activists and Journalists* is the final product of this extraordinary journalistic journey. The edition rests in the journalistic hands of Gloria Muñoz Ramirez and David Avendaño Mendoza (Krizna), a transgender sex worker of the Mexican Network of Sexual Work. It is co-authored by four sex workers – Beatriz Herrera, Patricia Mérida Ortiz, Sandra Montiel Díaz and María Soledad Sánchez Toledo. They interviewed and edited the stories of the 16 sex workers.

The book is a powerful and moving testimony of women, the elderly, Central American migrants, transgender sex workers, HIV carriers and indigenous people with different stories of violence, family breakdown, exploitation and discrimination. In the 199 pages are personal histories of broken relationships, sexual exploitation, human trafficking, discrimination against transgender sex workers, alcoholism and drug addiction. The stories revolve around the questions that journalists almost never ask sex workers: their childhood, the machismo they face at home, the risk of sexual diseases, the violence of some clients and, above all, the reasons why they decided to put themselves on a street corner.

Whores, Journalist and Activists is a book – I would suggest – deeply rooted in two of the most fundamental journalistic genres in Latin America, 'la crónica' (the chronicles) and 'el testimonio' (the testimony). Both journalistic genres are deeply underpinned by personal stories and struggles and socio-political demands (Castillo 2015). In both genres the norms of objectivity are thrown out the window and the doors of subjectivity and activism are thrown wide open.

The book – and the seven years of journalistic training underpinning it – has deeply empowered sex workers. They see themselves as historical subjects able to reclaim the word 'whore' as a fighting banner in the struggle for their human rights. And they now recognise the agency that journalism and activism – the ensemble – has, in demanding respect, acceptance and recognition.

References

Castillo, Antonio (2015) The new Latin American journalistic crónica, emotions and hidden signs of reality, *Global Media Journal*, Vol. 9 No. 2 pp 1-12

Castillo, Moises (2016) CDMX: City of prostitution, *Siempre*, 11 October. Available online at http://www.siempre.mx/2016/10/cdmx-ciudad-de-prostitucion, accessed on 2 April 2019

Domínguez, Pedro (2016) In Mexico DF 70,000 work in prostitution, *Milenium*, 11 October. Available online at https://www.milenio.com/estados/en-la-cdmx-ejercen-prostitucion-70-mil, accessed on July 9 2019

Fong, Ting, Holroyd, Eleanor Anne and Wong, William C. W. (2013) Dangerous women of Hong Kong? Media construction of stigma in female sex workers, *Journal of Behavioural Health*, Vol. 2 No.1 pp 59-65

Gimeno, Beatriz (2013) Towards a new debate on prostitution, *beatrizgimeno.es*, 23 October. Available online at https://beatrizgimeno.es/2013/10/25/hacia-un-nuevo-debate-sobre-la-prostitucion, accessed on 20 February 2019

Lamas, Marta (2016) An end to the shame: Stigma and political participation among Mexican sex workers, *Open Democracy*, 9 December. Available online at https://www.opendemocracy.net/en/end-to-shame-stigma-and-political-participation-among-mexican-sex-workers, accessed on 10 March 2019

López, Magadalena, and Mestre, Ruth (2006) *Sex work. Recognize rights*, Valencia: La Burbuja Editors

Montejo, Jaime (2013) Sex work in Mexico, millionaire earnings and rights without recognizing, *Desinformémonos*, 3 January. Available online at https://desinformemonos.org/trabajo-sexual-en-mexico-ganancias-millonarias-y-derechos-sin-reconocer, accessed on 12 March 2019

Muñoz Ramirez, Gloria and Avendaño, David (2018) *Whores, Activists and Journalists*, Mexico City: Desinformémonos Editors

O'Delia, Lily (2016) Media coverage of sex workers erases our voices, *Medium*, 23 May. Available online at https://medium.com/the-establishment/media-coverage-of-sex-workers-erases-our-voices-84460ca6867b, accessed on 21 May 2019

Oppenheim, Maya (2019) Sex work to be decriminalised in Mexico City in bid to cut trafficking, *Independent*, 2 June. Available online at https://www.independent.co.uk/news/world/americas/mexico-city-sex-work-trafficking-decriminalised-congress-vote-a8940486.html, accessed 4 June 2019

Simón, Patricia and Saiz, Vanesa (2018) How journalism can help end the intractable prostitution conflict, *Letras Libres* September 13. Available online at https://www.letraslibres.com/espana-mexico/politica/como-acabar-desde-el-periodismo-el-conflicto-irresoluble-la-prostitucion, accessed on 3 March 2019

Note on the Author

Antonio Castillo, PhD, is a Latin American journalist and a senior journalism academic at RMIT University, in Melbourne, Australia. Antonio's research includes political journalism; journalism and activism; and narrative journalism.

Chapter 9

Confronting the Taboo of Homosexuality in 1980s Portugal

Manuel Coutinho examines the role journalism played in confronting the taboos surrounding homosexuality in Portugal during an era in which the conservative mores of the Salazar dictatorship were persisting.

Post-authoritarian Portugal

In 1965, Portugal was four years into a violent conflict to maintain sovereignty over its colonies of Angola, Guinea-Bissau and Mozambique. Amid national hysteria about conscription, growing illegal immigration, as well as increasing international pressure, the Portuguese dictator, António de Oliveira Salazar, ended up defining the nation's ideology and approach to this escalating situation with two words: 'Orgulhosamente sós' ('Proudly alone'). This was, in a way, the dominant view of the authoritarian regime that took down the First Republic in 1926, a regime that in 1933 became known as New State. This fascist government ruled Portugal with a strict belief of nation over individuality, while its people lived under the 'distraction' of the so-called 'triple F': Football, Fado, and Fátima (i.e. Catholicism). The 1974 revolution brought with it the end of the old regime and the promise of self-determination, freedom of speech and a nation open to the world. However, 1980s' Portugal was still largely dominated by the conservative agenda of its former regime and many issues were still the subject of taboo, social wariness and political scrutiny. Journalism was under similar constraints and, according to scholar Adriano Rodrigues, it was also going through a crisis that limited its scope, opportunity and relevance (Rodrigues 1980: 7).

From the many publications that tried to change the discourse in Portugal, *Cadernos de Reportagem* undoubtedly stands out due to its reportorial language, subject diversity and modern approach. Even though only six issues were published, scholar and journalist Jacinto

Godinho considers this a revolutionary work of Portuguese reportage (Godinho 2009). On the back of each issue there was a small editorial note that defined the publication as something 'between a newspaper and a book, harmonizing the accessibility of the first one with the profundity of the second', and addressing subjects that were 'not mentioned in the Portuguese press due to their boldness, marginality, provocation and defiance'. This definition does, indeed, capture the contents of *Cadernos de Reportagem* and its journalists' writing style. At the same time, this definition is, in part, reminiscent of Norman Sims's statement: 'Literary journalists are boundary crossers in search of a deeper perspective of our lives and times' (Sims 1995: 18-19). As this chapter aims to show, this Portuguese publication stands out amongst others of its time for its search for this 'deeper perspective' and its examination of complex subjects.

In fact, each issue of *Cadernos de Reportagem* was dedicated entirely to a different aspect of contemporary Portugal. The first of six issues, published in 1983, addressed Portuguese homosexuality; the second included a profile of Portuguese folk musician and political activist Zeca Afonso; the third reported on clandestine abortions; the fourth explored the world of esoteric rituals; the fifth presented a profile of a murderer in prison; while the last issue focused on those who came to Portugal from the former colonies after the 1974 revolution. With a small print run of just 7,500 copies per issue, *Cadernos de Reportagem* ceased publication in 1984 and its six main reporters – a different one for each issue – are known today mainly for other works.

While each issue tackled controversial topics in depth and challenged common misconceptions, it is the first issue that stands out the most. Addressing what at the time was still a substantially ignored subject by Portuguese media, reporter Guilherme de Melo focused on homosexuality in Portugal and the taboo surrounding it. The issue is still in many aspects relevant today. With close to 60 pages and 14 distinct chapters, the publication goes in-depth on a wide range of topics: from the false openness to homosexuality, to the relationship with the family and the need to revaluate gender definitions, among others. From the beginning, the journalist pulls the reader in by describing the following scene set at the docks between a teenager and an older man:

> The teenager stepped away from the wall he was leaning on and walked towards the man. ...

Cigarette? You ... cigarette...? he asks in a low voice [in English] accompanying his words by gesturing his fingers to his mouth. The man answers back with a smile.

You want a smoke, do you?

For a moment, there is surprise on the young man's face. Perhaps not surprise, perhaps a sudden disappointment.

Ah! You are Portuguese, says the teenager.

Would you prefer if I were a foreigner? asked the man.

Well, in a way... The teenager gestured with his thumb and his index. Foreigners always pay more, you know? (Melo 1983: 7-8).

This moment is followed by a scene where the younger man discusses how much money he wants to be paid for sex and, after a mutual agreement, the older man suggests a place for them to go. While this scene is not meant to represent homosexuality relations in general in Portugal at the time, it serves as a strong starting point while setting in motion the first topic addressed in Melo's article: secret sexual transactions. We later find out that this man has a wife and children and that this is not his first time having sex with a man. In his own words, the secrecy is kept because the family 'wouldn't understand' and everyone is better off 'living this lie'. This search for furtive sexual encounters with members of the same sex, while living a dual life, is thus represented in this scene as a justified necessity. The double life, and the compulsion to disguise it, is a recurrent theme across the article and, in general, most people interviewed by Melo state similar reasons. Consider, for example, a different and yet still distressing point of view of a pregnant woman interviewed in one of the latter chapters:

I am gay. I always have been ever since I can remember it. But I belong to a conservative Christian family. I dated and later married ... the society I belong to has a natural expectation for every women and men to do so. My truth lives only with me. ... Do you know what it is like to live your entire life frustrated? (ibid: 56).

The secrecy surrounding homosexuality, however, permeates other aspects of people's lives. In one of the first chapters, Melo describes an incident at a service shop. In this scene, a mechanic jokes around with his colleagues about a homosexual couple he had seen on the beach (ibid: 11). The reader has access to this scene through the eyes of one of the co-workers. While being interviewed, he vehemently states that he would never openly reveal his sexual orientation to his colleagues for fear of being fired. This fear, in his own words, is entirely justified since just months earlier two of his colleagues were pressured to resign after their co-workers became wary of their sexual orientation and forced their employer's hand. It is important to note that it was only in 1982 that homosexuality was decriminalised in Portugal while Melo's article was published soon afterwards – in June/July 1983.

The relationship with family and friends and the repercussions of coming out (often with grave consequences) are a recurrent theme of Melo's reporting. As he writes:

> Either they simply reject him, marginalizing him and humiliating him, or they would consider him sick and in need of treatment, no matter the cost. As if his body was not working properly and his parents needed to take him to the doctor ... but, in this case, the doctor was in fact substituted by prostitutes (ibid: 22-23).

This was what some parents believed was best in order to 'treat' a son who deviated from what was expected at the time in terms of sexual orientation. This 'solution' hoped that this loveless first sexual encounter would magically assert a son's hidden masculinity and leave behind any further doubts. No such 'solution' was open to women. During the New State dictatorship women were blocked from most jobs and careers, being expected merely to marry and become mothers. In addition, during the dictatorship there were few opportunities for women to escape unhappy marriages since, from 1940 to 1975, religious weddings could not be annulled according to state law (Câncio 2008). Moreover, to leave the country during the dictatorship, a wife needed a written authorisation by her husband. The impact of this patriarchal ideology continued years after the 1974 revolution and the end of the Portuguese dictatorship. In response to Melo's questions, a 25-year-old lesbian who lived with her widowed mother, her sister and her brother-in-law was quick to point out the differences between genders:

> On Saturday night, for example, I like to go out with friends, have a drink at someone's place or go to a nightclub. My mother and brother-in-law argue with me the following day if I happen to arrive after one in the morning. What if the neighbours saw me, what would they think? They'll think that it is not good for a single woman to arrive home so late. If I had a boyfriend or someone whom everyone knew that I would one

day marry, then that would be OK. .... To a man everything is permitted. In their logic, if a man arrives late it is because he was with a new lover and spent the night out with her. For a single man it is perfectly natural. ... It gives him prestige and is a matter of pride for the family (Melo op cit: 33-34).

In this sense, the social constraints and women's expected role limited her from birth. On the other hand this happens no matter her sexual orientation. This fact is not lost on Guilherme de Melo, who comments:

While life is not easy for male or female same-sex attraction, the truth is that the first one ... is able to enjoy more inherent advantages due to his gender (in a society where everything is permitted to a man while for a woman everything is still constrained) ... for a lesbian who wishes to be emancipated, she must first do so as a woman (ibid: 36).

Interestingly at this point in his article, Melo uses the subject of homosexuality and emancipation to make a comparison between it and the fight for women's rights at the time. In this way the journalist often deviates from his main subject to address the root of the problem. These efforts are meant to justify how we have come to this moment of repression and taboo in Portugal during the 1980s – years after the promises of freedom at the end of the dictatorial regime. At the same time, Melo presents an important and incisive vision of homosexuality. This becomes clear at different moments, such as when he considers the claims that more men and women were identifying as homosexual than ever before:

What grew was the knowledge of homosexuality. ... Censorship ceased to exist ... . Suddenly, the general public saw in front of them, flesh and bones, clear and real, the homosexual that before would live in seclusion. ... Debates and conferences openly discuss the subject of homosexuality (ibid: 42).

Melo also points to a different problem at the time: the damaging focus often on the matter of 'why'. As he explains:

Today's articles about homosexuality are still worried about explaining it instead of accepting it. Sociologists and doctors are still obsessively linking it to child traumas, controlling mothers or violent fathers. A similar reasoning is often used to try to explain why someone from a wealthy family would ever rob a bank or kill a person. This mindset perpetuates ... a homosexual as an outcast, a stranger, someone outside of normality in need of isolation and treatment ... (ibid: 57).

Conclusion: The Freedom to be Different

It is easy to forget the importance of articles such as Melo's given the deep changes that have occurred since then. *Cadernos de Reportagem*'s low circulation and its short-lived publication unfortunately make it difficult to assess the publication's direct impact and even harder to assess that of Melo's article. Still, in the second issue of this publication there is a small editorial note mentioning that the article was met with some scandal and that some bookstores had even refused to sell the publication (Teles 1983).

Thanks to its length, distinct topics and straightforward language, Melo's article stands out at a time when homosexuality was often the subject of bigotry and hate. These attitudes have fortunately changed throughout the past few decades and Portugal's progress was seen favorably in the *Special Eurobarometer 437: Discrimination in the EU in 2015* (2015: 61-62).

As a closing argument, consider Melo's final sentences:

> Last weekend I had lunch in a friends' house. .... When I was leaving the young couple walked me to the door to say goodbye ... . I was entering the elevator when I decided to turn around for a last wave goodbye. They were both together, next to the door, arms around each other's waist. And they kissed one another, sweetly, right when I turned to say goodbye. ... What I saw in them was kindness and love. ... A similar thing happened the other day with another couple ... what I saw was exactly the same. But that time, in front of my eyes, it was not a man and a woman – but two men. With their arms around each other's waist. Their lips searching in their partner's mouth the sweet taste that only lovers know. With the same expression of profound happiness. ... Both images of these happy couples were precisely the same. The thing that separated them, was the freedom to be different (Melo 1983: 58).

References

Araújo, David, Pinto, Filipe and Tomás, Sérgio (2014) *Desigualdades entre os homens e as mulheres antes do 25 de Abril* [*Inequalities between men and women before 25 April*], RTP, Available online at ensina.rtp.pt/artigo/o-ideal-feminino-do-estado-novo, accessed on 21 May 2019

Câncio, Fernanda (2008) *Breve história legal do casamento e do seu fim em Portugal* [*Brief legal history of marriage and its end in Portugal*], *Diário de Notícias*, 15 April. Available online at www.dn.pt/arquivo/2008/interior/breve-historia-legal-do-casamento-e-do-seu-fim-em-portugal-997861.html, accessed on 21 May 2019

Godinho, Jacinto (2009) *As Origens da Reportagem: Imprensa* [*The Origins of Reportage: Press*], Lisbon: Livros Horizonte

Melo, Guilherme de (1983) Ser homossexual em Portugal [To be a homosexual in Portugal], *Cadernos de Reportagem*, June/July pp 7-58

Neves, Helena and Calado, Maria (2001) *Estado Novo e as Mulheres: O Género como Investimento Ideológico e de Mobilização* [*New State and Women: Gender as a Mobilising and Ideological Investment*], Lisbon: Biblioteca Museu República e Resistência

Rodrigues, Adriano (1980) *Media and Journalism – A Comunicação Social*, Lisbon: Vega

Sims, Norman (1995) The art of literary journalism, Sims, Norman and Kramer, Mark (eds) *Literary Journalism*, New York: Ballantine Press pp 3-19

Telles, Viriato (1983) Zeca Afonso: As voltas de um andarilho [Zeca Afonso: The life of a wanderer] *Cadernos de Reportagem*, Agosto/Setembro pp 7-58

European Commission (2015) *Special Eurobarometer 437: Discrimination in the EU in 2015*. Available online at data.europa.eu/euodp/data/dataset/S2077_83_4_437_ENG, accessed on 21 May 2019

Note on the Author

Manuel João de Carvalho Coutinho is an independent researcher from Lisbon, Portugal. He is a conference speaker, a published academic and a content writer. His research interests include non-fiction, creative writing, journalism and literary journalism. He holds a Bachelor's Degree in Philosophy, a Master's in the Philosophy of Education and a Master's and a PhD in Science Communication in Media and Journalism. He is a fan of board games, books and artisanal beer, not necessarily in that order.

Chapter 10

Beyond the Dystopian Gloom: Orwell and Sexuality

George Orwell is normally associated with the doom and gloom of *Nineteen Eighty-Four*'s dystopian society. Yet, as Richard Lance Keeble argues, there is a life affirmative side to both his character and writings – and sexuality is very much part of that.

Susan Watson recalled that when Orwell invited Aunt Nellie Limouzin – wrapped in black satin and adorned with jet beads – to tea in Canonbury Square, he'd amuse her with his collection of postcards by Donald McGill. He told her not to serve tea until Nellie had finished laughing at the jokes (Meyers 2000: 268).

The central place of sexuality in the writings of George Orwell (too often associated with the gloom of his dystopian novel *Nineteen Eighty-Four*) has been mainly missed by critics and biographers. Feminist commentators such as Daphne Patai (1984), Beatrix Campbell (1984) and Deirdre Beddoe (1984) accuse Orwell of misogyny: rightly so. But as so often with Orwell (his character so complex and contradictory) there is another side which this chapter attempts to outline.

This chapter examines the role of sex in a selection of his works (*Down and Out in Paris and London, Homage to Catalonia* and 'Such, Such were the Joys'). Moreover, an analysis of *Nineteen Eighty-Four* demonstrates that the representation of Julia, who conducts a secret affair with the anti-hero Winston Smith, is far more nuanced than generally thought: Orwell lays quite a few hints that she is, indeed, a Party spy drawing Smith into a honeytrap. The chapter moves on to consider his 1941 *Horizon* essay on McGill's sexy seaside postcards. Orwell cleverly mixes attitudes of pleasure (captured, above all, in the humour of the sexy cartoons and his own writing) and *faux* shame. In the process, he explores with a lightness of touch (along with dollops of irony) such issues as the essential purpose of jokes, the notion of goodness, gender stereotypes – and the complexities of the human condition, no less (Keeble 2018).

The Feminist Critique

Feminist critics unite in condemning Orwell as a misogynist. According to Beatrix Campbell (1984: 131): 'Part of the problem is that Orwell's eye never comes to rest on the culture of women, their concerns, their history, their movements. He only holds women to the filter of his own desire – or distaste.' According to Deirdre Beddoe (1984: 140): 'Orwell was not only anti-feminist but he was totally blind to the role women were and are forced to play in the order of things.' And for Daphne Patai, author of the foundational *The Orwell Mystique: A Study in Male Ideology* (1984), Orwell cultivated 'a traditional notion of masculinity, complemented by a generalized misogyny' (ibid: 15). He 'polarizes human beings according to sex roles and gender identity and legitimizes male displays of dominance and aggression' (ibid: 17). John Newsinger is also critical of Orwell's attitudes to women. He writes (2018: 154): 'He regularly dismissed both "feminists" and "feminism". He was unfortunately one of those male socialists who were opposed to every oppression, except that of women.' Even Christopher Hitchens, hardly noted as a feminist, argues (2002: 105): 'Every one of the female characters [in his novels] is practically devoid of the least trace of intellectual or reflective capacity.'

Along with Orwell's representation of gender issues, his behaviour, sadly, could also at times be described as misogynistic. In a letter to a relative in 1972, Jacintha Buddicom, a childhood friend of the then-Eric Blair, writes: 'How I wish I had been ready for betrothal when Eric asked me to marry him on his return from Burma [in 1927]. He had ruined what had been such a close and fulfilling relationship since childhood by trying to take us the whole way before I was anywhere near ready for that' (Davison 2010: 9, cited in Bluemel 2012: 19). Bluemel (ibid) suggests that this substantiates the claim by Dione Venables, in a 'Postscript' to the reprint of Buddicom's memoir *Eric and US: A Remembrance of George Orwell* (2006 [1974]: 182), that he had come close to raping Buddicom. Biographer Bernard Crick also tells of the occasion in 1944 when Orwell accompanied a former BBC acquaintance home late one night after a party at William and Hetta Empson's house in Hampstead, north London, and while crossing the Heath, tried 'to make love to her far too persistently, somewhat violently even' (Crick 1980: 465). A few months later, Orwell made a 'vigorous pass' at Anne Popham (later to wed the art historian, Quentin

Bell) while he sat beside her on a bed in an Islington flat. Crick reports (ibid: 485) that Orwell 'said that he was very attracted to her, kissed her and asked if she would consider marrying him. Touched and flattered, though embarrassed and a little shocked by his dispassionate precipitancy, she disengaged herself...'. Later, he sent Popham two letters, not apologising but trying to explain his actions. In the first he wrote: 'It is only that I feel so desperately alone sometimes...' (ibid).

Orwell's Other Side

Orwell was a complex man with many sides to his personality. One was distinctly 'un-misogynistic'. This is perhaps not surprising: his mother, Ida (née Limouzin) was a feminist and his aunt Nellie (with whom he stayed occasionally while investigating the plight of the poor in London in the late 1920s and in the early 1930s when she moved to Paris) was to marry Eugène Adam, an ex-anarchist, Esperantist and founder member of the French Communist Party (Brennan 2017: 25).

Many of the women Orwell was later to be associated with (Jacintha Buddicom, Stevie Smith, Inez Holden, Mabel Fierz, Celia Kirwan – not to mention his two wives Eileen O'Shaughnessy and Sonia Brownell) were forceful characters who would hardly have tolerated a misogynist. As a father to Richard Horatio, whom he and Eileen adopted in June 1944, Orwell certainly confounded the expectations of his day, displaying considerable affection for the child, taking him for walks in the pram – and even changing his nappies (though with a cigarette in his mouth) (Crick 1980: 483).

Sexuality and *Down and Out*

Orwell was following a long line of socially-concerned writers (such as Jack London, James Greenwood, Charles Booth, Beatrix Potter) when between 1928 and 1931 he went 'down and out' and lived alongside the beggars and hop pickers. Significantly, his account of his experiences, the part fiction/part memoir *Down and Out in Paris and London* (1933) features sexuality prominently. The account starts with Charlie, a fellow Parisian down-and-out, boasting (somewhat offensively) of his sexual exploits, raping a prostitute in a brothel:

> Without another word I pulled her off the bed and threw her onto the floor. And then I fell upon her like a tiger! ... More and more savagely I renewed the attack. Again and again the girl tried to escape, she cried out for mercy anew, but I laughed at her (Orwell 1980 [1933]: 19).

One of the aspects of the book somewhat underplayed in critiques of the text to date is the way in which homosexuality is treated so openly: this at a time when it was illegal and taboos hindered any serious discussion of the subject. For instance, when reflecting on his experiences, Orwell argues that one of the 'great evils' of the tramp's life is that he is cut off entirely from contact with women (ibid: 115). He continues:

> It is obvious what results of this must be: homosexuality, for instance, and occasional rape cases. ...The sexual impulse, not to put it any higher, is a fundamental impulse, and starvation of it can be almost as demoralizing as physical hunger (ibid: 116).

Homage to Catalonia and Homoeroticism

Traditionally warfare is often seen as a site for male bonding (Keeble 2015a). Indeed, *Homage to Catalonia* (1962 [1938]), Orwell's account of his time spent fighting alongside Republican militiamen during the Spanish civil war in 1936-1937, begins with a description of a meeting at the Lenin barracks in Barcelona with an Italian soldier which, it could be argued, has a remarkably overt homoerotic element (Keeble 2015b: 213). Earlier, in Burma (from 1922-1927), attractive boys were of sexual interest to Eric Blair, according to John Sutherland (2016: 98-99).

Orwell's ambivalent attitudes towards homosexuality appear in his response to Oscar Wilde. Kristian Williams points out how Orwell expressed in his writings and letters his disdain for 'Nancy poets', 'pious sodomites' and the 'pansy left' (2017: 41). Yet, throughout his life, Orwell had a high opinion of Wilde's writings.

'Such, Such Were the Joys' (and Sorrows) of Sex!

Orwell's (partly fictionalised) memoir of his time at St Cyprian's prep school, near Eastbourne, between 1911 and 1917, 'Such, Such Were the Joys' (1970 [1952]) is remarkable for its sexual explicitness (Keeble 2018). At the start of Section IV there is a lengthy discussion of sex and homosexuality in particular. Sex becomes linked with secrecy, betrayal, ignorance, confusion and shame. Earlier, he reports how he 'sneaked' to his favourite teacher, Brown 'a suspected case of homosexuality' (1970 [1952]: 401). All this leads to an account (how true, how fictional?) of his own sex life and of the sexual development of youths in general. Orwell was never much impressed by psychoanalysis, as biographer Gordon Bowker stresses (Bowker 2003: 48). Yet, if openness about feelings and sexuality (making the personal political) is another mark of today's New Man, then Orwell was ahead of his times (Keeble 2018: 85). Here, he admits to being 'in an almost sexless state, which is normal or at any rate common in boys of that age' (1970 [1952]: 402). Carefully, he teases out the chronology of his sexual awakening. At five or six 'like many children' (so aiming to generalise from the personal), he moves through a period of sexuality.

> My friends were the plumber's children up the road and we used sometimes to play games of a vaguely erotic kind. One was called 'playing at doctors' and I remember getting a faint but definitely pleasant thrill from holding a toy trumpet, which was supposed to be a stethoscope, against a little girl's belly (ibid: 403).

Next, he falls deeply in love with a girl named Elsie. And he goes on to dwell on his boyhood sexual confusions with what appears compelling honesty (though it may well be all fiction). Most of the Facts of Life (those capital letters indicating their Importance and Severity) are learned through watching animals. The section climaxes with him noticing his penis sometimes standing of its own accord – and his feeling of shame (ibid).

The Julia Conundrum in *Nineteen Eighty-Four*

Sexual politics lie at the heart of *Nineteen Eighty-Four*. According to Cass R. Sunstein (2005: 241):

> Orwell suggests that totalitarian governments favour 'sexual puritanism', which induces 'hysteria', something that such governments mobilize in their own favour. This is the image of patriotic frenzy as 'sex gone sour'. On this view, sexual freedom embodies freedom and individualism, and it is the deepest enemy of a totalitarian state. A state that allows sexual freedom will be unable to repress its citizens.

Or, as Robin West stresses (2005: 248): 'Erotic sex. Winston Smith insists in *Nineteen Eighty-Four*, is a truly *political* and even revolutionary act.'

Yet, Orwell's representation of Julia, the woman who has a furtive affair with the anti-hero Winston Smith, draws particular wrath from feminist critics. For Patai, Orwell evokes yet another female stereotype in representing Julia as a rebel only 'from the waist downwards': she is motivated only by a love of sexual pleasure and is totally uninterested in the political dynamics of the society that oppresses her (Patai 1984: 243). When Winston reads to her from the book, supposedly written by the leader of the rebellion, Goldstein, she falls asleep (ibid: 244).

But what if Julia is actually a member of the Party, luring Winston Smith into a honeytrap? Gordon Bowker is one of the few critics to suspect Julia is actually not quite what she might appear – she could be:

> ... a dissembler leading Winston straight into the arms of the Thought Police. On Airstrip One, truth rests on ever-shifting sands, only pain and Room 101 are real. Such a reading gives the book a strangely modern character making it a novel about the slippery unstable nature of meaning (2003: 388-389).

Orwell offers various clues: when Smith first sees her, she is arriving at the Two Minutes Hate session with, of all people, O'Brien (who first befriends him – and then conducts the torture in Room 101) (Orwell 2000 [1949]: 12). When he is later leaving Charrington's shop, he sees Julia: 'There was no doubting any longer that the girl was spying on him. She must have followed him here...' (ibid: 115). Given this interpretation, Julia's falling asleep whilst Winston reads from Goldstein's *The Theory and Practice of Oligarchical Collectivism* is completely understandable (ibid: 247). As a Party spy she would find the book totally boring – and sleep-inducing.

Seeing Julia as a spy can lead to two further contrasting interpretations. On the one hand it can be seen as subverting the conventional image of her: instead of being a submissive sex object she becomes a highly politicised agent of the state, influencing events in major ways. Or, as Tim Crook (2018) argues: 'There is still a valid feminist criticism of this dimension of the characterisation in deploying and demeaning the woman as a stereotypical Mata Hari-type honeytrap where women feature almost exclusively as the corrupting and seducing agents of sexpionage.'

Orwell's Celebration of Sexy Seaside Postcards

One of Orwell's most original studies of popular culture focuses on the sexy seaside postcards of Donald McGill – published in Cyril Connolly's literary journal *Horizon* in September 1941. According to John Sutherland, Orwell began collecting these postcards at about the age of twelve (2016: 77). In order to win over the somewhat highbrow readers of *Horizon*, Orwell begins cleverly by expressing *faux* shame:

> Your first impression is of overpowering vulgarity. This is quite apart from the ever-present obscenity and apart also from the hideousness of the colours. They have an utter lowness of mental atmosphere which comes not only in the nature of the jokes but,

even more, in the grotesque, staring blatant quality of the drawings (Orwell 1962 [1941]: 143).

But none of this outrage prevents Orwell from pressing on to analyse the content. First, he identifies the main subject areas: sex, home life, drunkenness, WC jokes, inter-working class snobbery and stock figures. Then he moves on to translate the real pleasure he derives from the sexy images and jokes into a profound discussion of the deeper social, class, moral and psychological aspects of the postcards. 'The postcards,' he suggests, 'give expression to the Sancho Panza view of life' – which Orwell goes on to endorse unreservedly.

> The Don Quixote-Sancho Panza combination ... is simply the ancient dualism of body and soul in fiction form ... If you look into your own mind, which are you, Don Quixote or Sancho Panza? Almost certainly you are both. There is one part of you that wishes to be a hero or a saint, but another part of you is a little fat man who seeks very clearly the advantages of staying alive with a white skin. He is your unofficial self, the voice of the belly protesting against the soul (op cit: 151-152).

Orwell ends the essay in a droll, witty, aphoristic sort of way: 'On the whole, human beings want to be good, but not too good, and not quite all the time' (ibid: 154).

Conclusion

Orwell's representations of gender have long interested academics. His treatment of sexuality, in contrast, is little covered by Orwellian commentators. Yet this chapter argues that sex lies at the core of much of Orwell's writings. The gloomy, dystopian vision of *Nineteen Eighty-Four*, his most celebrated novel, probably helps create a public image of Orwell as a gloomy, pessimistic, humourless and – in the context of this paper – a rather unsexual man. In fact, the opposite is the case. For his times, Orwell was remarkably open about sexual matters, even his homoerotic tendencies – and the development of his own sexuality.

References

Beddoe, Deirdre (1984) Hindrance and help-meets: Woman in the writings of George Orwell, Norris, Christopher (ed.) *Inside the Myth: Orwell: Views from the Left*, London: Lawrence and Wishart pp 139-154

Bluemel, Kristin (2012) The intimate Orwell: Women's production, feminist consumption, Keeble, Richard Lance (ed.) *Orwell Today*, Bury St Edmunds: Abramis pp 15-29

Bowker, Gordon (2003) *George Orwell*, London: Little, Brown

Brennan, Michael G. (2017) *George Orwell and Religion*, London and New York: Bloomsbury

Buddicom, Jacintha (2006 [1974]) *Eric and US: A Remembrance of George Orwell*, UK: Finlay Publishers, revised edition edited by Venables, Dione

Campbell, Beatrix (1984) Orwell: Paterfamilias or Big Brother?, Norris, Christopher (ed.) *Inside the Myth: Orwell: Views from the Left*, London: Lawrence and Wishart pp 128-136

Crick, Bernard (1980) *George Orwell: A Life*, Harmondsworth, Middlesex: Penguin

Crook, Tim (2018) On Julia and sexpionage, in an email to the author, 20 September 2018

Davison, Peter (ed.) (2010) *George Orwell: A Life in Letters*, London and New York: Penguin

Hitchens, Christopher (2002) *Orwell's Victory*, London: Allen Lane, The Penguin Press

Keeble, Richard Lance (2015a) Homage to literary journalism, *orwellsocietyblog*, 24 November. Available online at https://orwellsocietyblog.wordpress.com/2015/11/24/homage-to-literary-journalism-in-homage/, accessed on 15 August 2018

Keeble, Richard Lance (2015b) Orwell and the war reporter's imagination, Keeble, Richard Lance (ed.) *George Orwell Now!*, New York: Peter Lang pp 209-224

Keeble, Richard Lance (2018) 'The art of Donald McGill': Orwell and the pleasures of sex, *George Orwell Studies*, Vol 3, No. 1 pp 21-36

Meyers, Jeffrey (2000) *Orwell: Wintry Conscience of a Generation*, New York and London: W. W. Norton and Company Ltd

Newsinger, John (2018) *Hope Lies in the Proles: George Orwell and the Left*, London: Pluto Press

Orwell, George (1980 [1933]) *Down and Out in Paris and London, George Orwell: Complete and Unabridged*, London: Secker and Warburg/Octopus pp 15-120

Orwell, George (1962 [1938]) *Homage to Catalonia,* Harmondsworth, Middlesex: Penguin

Orwell, George (1962 [1941]) The Art of Donald McGill, *Decline of the English Murder and Other Essays,* Harmondsworth, Middlesex: Penguin pp 142-154

Orwell, George (2000 [1949]) *Nineteen Eighty-Four,* London: Penguin Classics

Patai, Daphne (1984) *The Orwell Mystique: A Study in Male Ideology,* Amherst: University of Massachusetts Press

Sunstein, Cass R. (2005) Sexual freedom and political freedom, Gleason, Abbott, Goldsmith, Jack and Nussbaum, Martha C. (eds) *On* Nineteen Eighty-Four: *Orwell and Our Future,* Princeton: Princeton University Press pp 233-241

Sutherland, John (2016) *Orwell's Nose: A Pathological Biography,* London: Reaktion Books

West, Robin (2005) Sex, law, power and community, Gleason, Abbott, Goldsmith, Jack and Nussbaum, Martha C. (eds) *On* Nineteen Eighty-Four: *Orwell and Our Future,* Princeton: Princeton University Press pp 242-260

Williams, Kristian (2017) *Between the Bullet and the Lie: Essays on Orwell,* Chico, Oakland, Edinburgh, Baltimore: AK Press

Chapter 11

Sex and Class in the Journalism of Moa Martinson

Sexuality and its consequences became a metaphor for the class
struggle in the journalism of the Swedish working class writer, Moa
Martinson (1890-1964). Anna Hoyles explores this through two
examples of Martinson's work: one a sober look at the consequences
of a lack of contraception and education, and the other a light-
hearted satire on the sexual mores of the middle and upper classes.

Introduction

Moa Martinson is a writer best known in Sweden for her modernist,
often semi-autobiographical novels. She is perceived as being part of
the proletarian school of Swedish literature due to her depiction of
working class women's lives. Several of her twenty books, published
between 1933 and 1959, were criticised for showing a poverty that
reviewers preferred to believe did not exist, as well as for their
portrayal of women's sexuality. Martinson's description of childbirth
and of women's sexual desire, as well as of marital rape, led to
accusations of a 'below the waist viewpoint' (Witt-Brattström 1989:
104).

While a large selection of Martinson's novels are still in print in Sweden
today, her journalism is little known, despite her prolificacy. Before her
debut novel, Martinson published from November 1922 more than
200 articles, letters, poems and reviews in the anarchist, syndicalist,
socialist, feminist and local press. Subsequently, she published less
frequently, but still almost 100 pieces of newspaper writing, including
40 as a regular columnist in the popular Social Democratic magazine,
Folket i Bild, during the 1950s.

Martinson's writing life spanned the desperately poor period of the
1920s pre-welfare state (when she wrote some of her most impassioned
political pieces) to the Social Democratic 'folkhem' (people's home) of
the 1960s, when Sweden's economy was booming, and it appeared to

be a country of equality and justice. In some senses Martinson's own life followed this trajectory: by the 1950s, she was seen as a national treasure, yet she always remained an outsider, commenting on society from below.

Martinson's newspaper work is often highly autobiographical – as are her novels – reflecting her life as a working class mother of five. It is upon this, as well as her activism (she was a member of the syndicalist organisation, SAC) that she bases much of her credibility. She bears witness to the poverty and injustice surrounding her (that affecting her own family, but also her friends and neighbours) and is unapologetically subjective. She claims authority on the basis of her social class and life experiences, including being part of the collective of working class women with which she self-identifies. She did not temper her feelings in her work, inspiring strong reactions, both positive and negative, in her readership.

Martinson's style is varied and she adopts different writing personas (see Witt-Brattström 1989; Hoyles 2012a) depending on subject and mood. She also explores the subject of sexuality from several perspectives. This chapter only touches upon two of them, but others range from defending the right of young single women not to be 'sexless angels' (Martinson 1930), to the discomfort she felt as a mother sitting in the cinema with her 'half-grown sons' watching an American film entitled *Lust*. Although the latter article is, in fact, a call to boycott American films for the sake of the executed anarchists Sacco and Vanzetti, the overwhelming impression caused by the article is one of excruciating embarrassment.

Eric Hobsbawm argues that the labour movement represented women as 'figures of suffering and endurance' (Hobsbawm 1978: 127) and this is a role Martinson willingly enters into and consigns others to. It is within this context that sexuality is discussed in the first part of this chapter. However, she could also be chatty and light-hearted. This contrasting style is the subject of the second part, where in character as her alter-ego Madam Andersson, in whose name Martinson wrote ten newspaper columns in 1925, she gives a humorous twist to otherwise serious subjects.

Bearing Witness to Working Class Women's Lives

In the spring of 1923, Martinson contributed several articles to a debate, in the syndicalist newspaper *Arbetaren,* on the subjects of abortion and contraception, both of which were then illegal. Initially

Martinson has conflicting views on the issues and her writing is contradictory; this is exemplified in an article from 15 April 1923. Here Martinson clearly cannot reconcile her knowledge that women are being worn out by childbearing with the fear, common within some parts of the labour movement at the time, that the use of contraception will wipe out the 'thinking' working class. It was thought that these women would use their knowledge of contraception to limit their offspring, who would then be absorbed into the middle class, while the 'lower' elements of the working class would not make use of the information and so would produce an 'endless' and 'deficient' proletariat (Levin 1997: 20).

Martinson takes this to heart as she writes of the danger that 'thousands of slow-witted worker's wives, who in their relationships to their husbands are worse than slaves, who even think it "sinful" to limit the production of children – yes, they would still fill the mines and factories with their progeny' (Helga 1923).

Martinson subsequently abandons her eugenics-centred arguments. The majority of the article focuses on the cruelties inflicted on working class women by the current system. Martinson draws upon her personal experiences to present a dark picture of working class women's lot, where men take no responsibility for the results of their sexual behaviour. The veracity of Martinson's examples are accentuated by details given, such as that of place. 'There is,' she writes, 'an estate 3 miles from my home' and then goes on to tell that one of the land worker's wives there:

> ... has given birth to fourteen children. Three times she has been admitted to Konradsberg [a psychiatric hospital] as totally insane and three times the doctors there have caused her to miscarry. Then she has been sent home without even an admonition to the husband. After a time she has again become pregnant, and melancholy and strangeness, due to her condition, have followed. However, if she has not become too unmanageable, she has been allowed to stay at home and give birth to living children with this terrible inheritance: insanity in the blood! (ibid).

In the same article, Martinson gives the example of a second neighbour who has given birth to seven children, all of whom were delivered using surgical instruments and who died shortly afterwards. Martinson witnesses several of these births and can, therefore, give a gripping, eyewitness account of the woman's plight. The situation is made worse by the fact that she cannot have an anaesthetic due to a heart problem. 'Every time I met the mother's eyes, filled with fear and pain, while the doctor prepared his work with the unborn child and his instruments, I was filled with hatred. I could have strangled the doctor.' Martinson blames the physician for refusing to help the woman with contraception or sterilisation. He is motivated, she believes, by the facts that it 'was an interesting case and the fee, despite the poverty, was good' (ibid).

In this, and other writing on the same subject, Martinson is unequivocal in her depiction of working class women as sexual victims of the class system and of men (of all classes). In these articles, there is little room for nuance. In contrast, in her persona as the garrulous charwoman Madam Andersson, Martinson takes a different and more satirical approach to sexuality.

The Charwoman's Viewpoint

Madam Andersson appears in the sexual educator, Elise Ottesen-Jensen's (Ottar), short-lived feminist magazine *Vi Kvinnor* (*We Women*) in 1925. When the first Madam Andersson column is introduced in the fourth issue of *Vi kvinnor*, it is ostensibly authored by Malla Andersson, a woman of all work – who scrubs, bakes, launders and milks cows. The fictional Madam is a character with a strong political ethos, who shows an irreverence towards both the political left and right, along with a desire to communicate the working class woman's perspective on events. She speaks her mind in public despite the impediments, she perceives, of both her gender and class and depicts life as she experiences it. Madam Andersson has, in common with her creator, a loquacious, easy tone addressing the reader intimately. She discusses subjects as varied as the indecency of young women's clothing and the issue of domestic abuse, all the while providing illustrative examples through a running commentary of life in her country village.

Recurrent characters include her best friend Fina, who likes the outspoken Malla, but also prefers to stay on the right side of the gossips in the village who are less admiring of the radical washerwoman. One of these is Johanna in Vångby, the archetype of a 'gadding gossip' (Tebbutt 1995: 22-23). Johanna is unmarried, a Pentecostalist and can speak 'foreign'. The latter is a cause of chagrin for Malla for she is unable to do so and her husband claims that a 'good' article needs to contain non-Swedish words. A whole column is devoted to the time that Johanna finds out that Madam Andersson is a published writer.

From then on Johanna excludes Malla from her coffee parties where she mocks the latter's compositions in front of the other neighbours – maintaining that her own poem, on the subject of 'heaven and harps', is by contrast a true work of art. She insultingly adds that 'at least' Andersson, Malla's husband, appreciates an 'educated woman' – meaning herself (Andersson 1925a). Unfortunately, the neighbours agree with Johanna's literary judgement. Despite her godly pretensions, Johanna's sexual morality leaves something to be desired. Madam Andersson is particularly upset that, when her husband is at Johanna's building her a brick stove, the latter changes her apron and curls her hair every day.

In tone, Madam Andersson differs from Martinson's other work and from the somewhat earnest emphasis of *Vi kvinnor* as a whole. The aim of the magazine is to educate women, particularly on matters of sexual health but also on class politics. As a consequence it publishes edifying novellas where virtuous women die in garrets after being driven to prostitution and family men take to drink due to the ills of capitalism. *Vi kvinnor* includes the writing of the celebrated American writer and progressive campaigner Upton Sinclair (1878-1968) on a number of occasions. His subjects range from the benefits of starvation cures (1925b), to marriage (1925a), to the sexual depravity of the wealthy (1925c). In the latter article, Sinclair dwells disapprovingly and at some length on orgies, wife swapping and the white slave trade. Malla, though firm in her opinions, favours a slightly more subtle approach. Where Sinclair is apparently morally indignant, whilst providing prurient details, Madam Andersson is amusing when making the same point.

Middle Class Morals

Madam Andersson gives three examples of sexual morality. The first is when the summer guests come to her village. They are obviously richer than the locals, whom they consider quaint, but are at pains to explain that they are just 'normal workers'. One woman earns Malla's scorn by not seeing the difference between a cow and a bull and then compounds the impression given of her ignorance by asserting that her husband receives high wages, not due to a good trade union, as Madam Andersson presumes, but because 'he's just very good at his job'. It transpires that her spouse is a factory doorman who registers the workers as they arrive for work and writes up '"even if they're only 3 minutes late. The managers are so pleased with him"' (Andersson 1925b). Madam Andersson is forced to walk away in disgust at this class betrayal. She later sees the wife kissing the local bookkeeper and the doorman out boating with Johanna, and concludes that there is a difference 'between workers and "workers"' (ibid). Clearly people who believe it is acceptable to betray their comrades do not have any other morals either.

Three magazine issues later Madam Andersson makes the same point, but this time skewering the hypocrisies of the wealthy and highlighting both gender and class inequalities. Malla tells of the day when, brought in to do the washing at the house of the railway director, she is working with his maid when the director himself comes in and starts shouting at and shaking the maid 'until her hairpins fell out' (Andersson 1925d). It transpires that he has lost his pipe and blames her for tidying it away. The pipe later emerges in the governess's room – 'they went through governesses at a terrible rate in that house'. The director's wife retires to bed weeping and the director himself comes down to the maids with a plate of strawberries, by way of apology, and is 'as nice as pie', but Madam Andersson is not fooled:

> That's the worst thing about the rich, you don't know when to like them least, when they shout, or when they're friendly. It's like being a dog which gets kicked when people are in a bad mood and a bone (as dogs don't particularly like strawberries) when they're in a good mood and is then expected to sit up and beg and forget about the kick (Andersson 1925d).

Although Madam Andersson and the servant feel pity for the director's wife they know that there is no solidarity to be found there. A children's maid at the house, who rejects the director's advances and goes to his wife for support, is harangued and immediately made to leave her position.

We are invited to observe the power imbalance in the class system, with the unreliable rich controlling the narrative in life. It is clear we should censor the railway director – who follows his whims while his wife and the women who work for him suffer – and at first to also cordially dislike Johanna. Yet, when Fina reveals to Madam Andersson that all the neighbours believe that Johanna has 'got herself in that way' and are guessing that the father is the doorman, mentioned two issues before (Andersson 1925c), Malla disappoints her friend. Despite luring Fina over, by baking a cake, to discuss yet another coffee party to which she is not invited – 'I'm no more than human, I wanted to know what they had said at Johanna's' – Madam Andersson declines to take gossipy pleasure in the details of her neighbour's misfortune.

'Yes, but you have to feel sorry for her,' I said, 'she feels sick, and there's no father for the kid, if she actually has one, think what a child that will be. Poor Johanna, that'll be her punishment. A puffed-up fool of a father, who makes trouble for people who are a few minutes late and a gossip of a mother, who gets around, it would probably be better that he wasn't born' (ibid).

Fina is disgusted by this reaction: '"You're so odd, Malla," said Fina. "So that one can't stand you, everybody says so."' Here Madam Andersson/Martinson rejects hyperbole and the role of gossip; it is easy to imagine what a different author in *Vi kvinnor* would make of the story. Instead, Malla gives a down-to-earth and compassionate reaction. Although she still censors pomposity, gossip and a lack of class consciousness, unlike the director's wife, Madam Andersson (and Martinson) consider female solidarity with the concerns of a single mother of overriding importance.

Conclusion

Despite the very different tone of the two types of writing discussed in this chapter they share similar ideas. For Martinson, the injustice of the class system and of gender imbalance, and the need for solidarity and new ways of thinking are perennial themes.

References

Andersson, Madam (Martinson, Moa) (1925a) Madam Anderssons spalt [Madam Andersson's Column], *Vi kvinnor*, No. 6 p. 15

Andersson, Madam (Martinson, Moa) (1925b) Madam Anderssons spalt [Madam Andersson's Column], *Vi kvinnor*, No. 12 p. 13

Andersson, Madam (Martinson, Moa) (1925c) Madam Anderssons spalt [Madam Andersson's Column], *Vi kvinnor*, No. 14 p. 8

Andersson, Madam (Martinson, Moa) (1925d) Madam Anderssons spalt [Madam Andersson's Column],*Vi kvinnor*, No. 15 p. 13

Chapman, Jane, Hoyles, Anna, Kerr, Andrew and Sherif, Adam (2015) *Comics and the World Wars: A Cultural Record*, Basingstoke: Palgrave Macmillan

Helga (Martinson, Moa) (1923) Fri och offentlig fosterdrivning [Free and Public Abortion], *Arbetaren*, 14 April p. 10

Hoyles, Anna (2012a) Rapport från en städhink 1925: Moa Martinsons Madam Andersson-kåserier [A Report from a Mop

Bucket 1925: Moa Martinson's Madam Andersson Columns], *I Moas sak - Sällskapet Moas Vänners skriftserie*, No. 11

Hoyles, Anna (2012a) Pickled Herrings and Politics: The Early Journalism of Moa Martinson, Keeble, Richard Lance and Tulloch, John (eds) *Global Literary Journalism*, New York, Oxford: Peter Lang pp 72-88

Levin, Hjördis (1997) *Kvinnorna på barrikaden* [Women on the Barricade], Stockholm: Carlssons

Martinson, Helga (Martinson, Moa) (1930) Kroppar och själar – Laura Petri gör succé i borgarpressen [Bodies and Souls – Laura Petri Becomes a Success in the Bourgeois Press], *Brand*, p. 5

Sinclair, Upton (1925a) Äktenskapet [Marriage]. *Vi kvinnor*, 15 August-1 September p. 5

Sinclair, Upton (1925b) Att svälta sig frisk [To Starve yourself Well], *Vi kvinnor*, 15 July-1 August p. 9

Sinclair, Upton (1925c) Överklassens degeneration och förfall i Amerika [The Upper Classes' Degeneration and Decline] *Vi kvinnor*, 1-15 March p. 8

Tebbutt, Melanie (1995) *Women's Talk? A Social History of 'Gossip' in Working Class Neighbourhoods, 1880-1960*, Aldershot: Scolar Press

Witt-Brattström, Ebba (1989) *Moa Martinson – Skrift och drift i trettiotalet* [*Moa Martinson – Writing and Desire in the Thirties*], Göteborg: Norstedts

Note on the Author

Anna Hoyles lives in Gothenburg, has recently completed her PhD on the literary journalism of Moa Martinson and has previously published on Martinson (Hoyles 2012a; 2012b). As research assistant, on the AHRC funded 'Comics and the World Wars: A Cultural Record', at the University of Lincoln, she also researched socialist newspaper comic strips from the First and Second World Wars (Chapman et al. 2015).

Conclusion

On the Need to Shed Academic Blinkers

Sue Joseph and Richard Lance Keeble

Lee Gutkind's longform online magazine *Creative Nonfiction* #71, entitled *Let's Talk about Sex*, appeared in 2019 containing several well-crafted and explicit longform stories about sex, love and romance. Significantly, Gutkind writes:

> … these stories depict sexually explicit and mostly hidden slices of real life. And I must say that, after editing CREATIVE NONFICTION for twenty-five years, I am surprised – and pleased. This and many other literary publications could never – would never – have published these essays twenty-five years ago. Perhaps not even ten years ago. We would have feared losing some of our audience and perhaps our financial supporters (2019).

He claims the reasons why there is a dearth of explicit sex life stories is because publishers have always had to be 'careful and cautious'. He explains:

> You could go off the deep end with poetry and fiction – one could always say poets and fiction writers were being imaginative, expansive, fantastical, improbable, way-out, etc. But nonfiction stories touched a nerve. Real people, real problems, real names. Too much information? Too personal? Too close to home? (ibid).

But is it too much information? Too personal? Too close to home? as Gutkind asks. Or perhaps it is one of a few final societal taboos that journalists and academics need to make more commonplace to report on, discuss and evaluate. Talking more about sex and consent and love and romance, in real terms, should educate and inform, rather than shock and titillate. Indeed, with this text, we are inviting a shedding of academic blinkers.

Reference

Gutkind, Lee (2019) What's the Story #71, From the Editor, *Creative Nonfiction*, Issue 71. Available online at https://www.creativenonfiction.org/online-reading/whats-story-71

Bite-Sized Public Affairs Books are designed to provide insights and stimulating ideas that affect us all in, for example, journalism, literature, social policy, education, government and politics.

They are deliberately short, easy to read, and authoritative books written by people who are either on the front line or who are informed observers. They are designed to stimulate discussion, thought and innovation in all areas of public affairs. They are all firmly based on personal experience and direct involvement and engagement.

The most successful people all share an ability to focus on what really matters, keeping things simple and understandable. When we are faced with a new challenge most of us need quick guidance on what matters most, from people who have been there before and who can show us where to start. As Stephen Covey famously said, "The main thing is to keep the main thing, the main thing."

But what exactly is the main thing?

Bite-Sized books were conceived to help answer precisely that question crisply and quickly and, of course, be engaging to read, written by people who are experienced and successful in their field.

The brief? Distil the 'main things' into a book that can be read by an intelligent non-expert comfortably in around 60 minutes. Make sure the book enables the reader with specific tools, ideas and plenty of examples drawn from real life. Be a virtual mentor.

We have avoided jargon – or explained it where we have used it as a shorthand – and made few assumptions about the reader, except that they are literate and numerate, involved in understanding social policy, and that they can adapt and use what we suggest to suit their own, individual purposes. Most of all the books are focused on understanding and exploiting the changes that we witness every day but which come at us in what seems an incoherent stream.

They can be read straight through at one easy sitting and then referred to as necessary – a trusted repository of hard won experience.

Bite-Sized Books Catalogue

Business Books

Ian Benn
    Write to Win
        How to Produce Winning Proposals and RFP
        Responses
Matthew T Brown
    Understand Your Organisation
        An Introduction to Enterprise Architecture Modelling
David Cotton
    Rethinking Leadership
        Collaborative Leadership for Millennials and Beyond
Richard Cribb
    IT Outsourcing: 11 Short Steps to Success
        An Insider's View
Phil Davies
    How to Survive and Thrive as a Project Manager
        The Guide for Successful Project Managers
Paul Davies
    Developing a Business Case
        Making a Persuasive Argument out of Your Numbers
Paul Davies
    Developing a Business Plan
        Making a Persuasive Plan for Your Business
Paul Davies
    Contract Management for Non-Specialists
Paul Davies
    Developing Personal Effectiveness in Business
Paul Davies
    A More Effective Sales Team
        Sales Management Focused on Sales People

Stuart Haining
    The Great Pension Pantomime
        It's All a Scam – Oh Yes It Is – Oh No It Isn't
Christopher Hosford
    Great Business Meetings! Greater Business Results
        Transforming Boring Time-Wasters into Dynamic
        Productivity Engines
Ian Hucker
    Risk Management in IT Outsourcing
        9 Short Steps to Success
Alan Lakey
    Idiocy in Commercial Life
        Practical Ways to Navigate through Nonsense
Marcus Lopes and Carlos Ponce
    Retail Wars
        May the Mobile be with You
Maiqi Ma
    Win with China
        Acclimatisation for Mutual Success Doing Business
        with China
Elena Mihajloska
    Bridging the Virtual Gap
        Building Unity and Trust in Remote Teams
Rob Morley
    Agile in Business
        A Guide for Company Leadership
Gillian Perry
    Managing the People Side of Change
        Ten Short Steps to Success in IT Outsourcing
Art Rain
    The Average Wage Millionaire
        Can Anyone Really Get Rich?
Saibal Sen
    Next Generation Service Management
        An Analytics Driven Approach
Don Sharp
    Nothing Happens Until You Sell Something
        A Personal View of Selling Techniques

Lifestyle Books

Anna Corthout
>Alive Again
>>My Journey to Recovery

Anna Corthout
>Mijn Tweede Leven
>>Kruistocht naar herstel

Phil Davies
>Don't Worry Be Happy
>>A Personal Journey

Phil Davies
>Feel the Fear and Pack Anyway
>>Around the World in 284 Days

Stuart Haining
>My Other Car is an Aston
>>A Practical Guide to Ownership and Other Excuses to Quit Work and Start a Business

Stuart Haining
>After the Supercar
>>You've Got the Dream Car – But Is It Easy to Part With?

Stuart Haining
>Alfa Male
>>. . If You're Brave Enough

Bill Heine
>Cancer
>>Living Behind Enemy Lines Without a Map

Regina Kerschbaumer
>Yoga Coffee and a Glass of Wine
>>A Yoga Journey

Gillian Perry
>Capturing the Celestial Lights
>>A Practical Guide to Imagining the Northern Lights

Arthur Worrell
>A Grandfather's Story
>>Arthur Worrell's War

Public Affairs Books

David Bailey, John Mair and Neil Fowler (Editors)
   Keeping the Wheels on the Road – Brexit Book 3
      UK Auto Post Brexit
Eben Black
   Lies Lobbying and Lunch
      PR, Public Affairs and Political Engagement – A Guide
Paul Davies, John Mair and Neil Fowler
   Will the Tory Party Ever Be the Same? – Brexit Book 4
      The Effect of Brexit
John Mair and Neil Fowler (Editors)
   Oil Dorado
      Guyana's Black Gold
John Mair and Richard Keeble (Editors)
   Investigative Journalism Today:
      Speaking Truth to Power
John Mair and Neil Fowler (Editors)
   Do They Mean Us – Brexit Book 1
      The Foreign Correspondents' View of the British
      Brexit
John Mair, Alex De Ruyter and Neil Fowler (Editors)
   The Case for Brexit – Brexit Book 2
John Mair, Richard Keeble and Farrukh Dhondy (Editors)
   V.S Naipaul:
      The legacy
John Mills
   Economic Growth Post Brexit
      How the UK Should Take on the World
John Redwood
   We Don't Believe You
      Why Populists and the Establishment See the World
      Differently
Christian Wolmar
   Wolmar for London
      Creating a Grassroots Campaign in a Digital Age

Fiction

Paul Davies
    The Ways We Live Now
        Civil Service Corruption, Wilful Blindness, Commercial
        Fraud, and Personal Greed – a Novel of Our Times
Paul Davies
    Coming To
        A Novel of Self-Realisation
Victor Hill
    Three Short Stories
        Messages, The Gospel of Vic the Fish, The Theatre of
        Ghosts

Children's Books

Chris Reeve – illustrations by Mike Tingle
    The Dictionary Boy
        A Salutary Tale
Fredrik Payedar
    The Spirit of Chaos
        It Begins

Printed in Great Britain
by Amazon